EXODUS
FROM THE DOOR OF NO RETURN

JOURNEY OF AN AMERICAN FAMILY

BY

ROY G. PHILLIPS, PhD

Edited by
Tsitsi D. Wakhisi

Introduction by
Former U.S. Representative Carrie P. Meek

authorHOUSE®

AuthorHouse™
1663 Liberty Drive, Suite 200
Bloomington, IN 47403
www.authorhouse.com
Phone: 1-800-839-8640

First published by AuthorHouse 1/23/2009

ISBN: 978-1-4389-0349-1 (sc)
ISBN: 978-1-4389-0348-4 (hc)

Printed in the United States of America
Bloomington, Indiana

This book is printed on acid-free paper.

Contents

ACKNOWLEDGEMENTS

T his book is a product of information collected from parents, grandparents, relatives and others who shared the family history and the story of the West African slave trade with me. It also includes the research of the U.S. Census, genealogical records, as well as information regarding plantations and slave owners who were cited as the owners of my ancestors. It has been an arduous and exciting journey to uncover the history of my family.

I wish to acknowledge those who shared the oral history of the family and the story of West African slavery with me: my maternal grandmother Mama Caroline Lee/Warren/Green (1882-1984); paternal adopted grandmother, Big Mama Lula Hamilton/Phillips (1877-1944); family friend Mattie Banks/Green (1886 - 1986); cousin Safronia Thornton/Gage (1882-1982); and the Rev. Jonah Parker, Growing Valley Colored Elementary-Junior High School principal (1912-2003).

I also acknowledge the following persons who contributed to this writing: cousin Pairlee Gooding/Rice (1910) and her daughter, cousin Levada Rice/Mitchell; Uncle S.J. Waller (1900); cousin Arless Willis/Brown (1912); cousin Hosie A. Gooding and Chief Nana Kweku Egyir Gyepi III, senior divisional chief of Cape Coast, Ghana, who shared the history of West African slavery and the Cape Coast Castle as well as original photos of the Door of No Return; Carol Hill de Santos, library specialist and Faedra Wills, genealogy librarian, Shreve Memorial Library, Shreveport, Louisiana; McDade family descendants: Gretchen Benner of Shreveport, Betty McDade, of Brenham, Texas, Attorney David Moore, Shreveport, Louisiana; and Willie Griffin, President of Ark-LA-Tex Genealogical Society, Inc., Shreveport, Louisiana.

Special thanks to my wife Vira, who spent many hours recalling special highlights of our 46 years in marriage and assisting in writing; Tsitsi D. Wakhisi, for providing outstanding editorial assistance; and Monique Harris and Gwendolyn Cayard for typing and revising the manuscript and the book cover design. Also, James and Silvia Hunter assisted with digital photography and Obaaye Abisobo and her daughter Wendy provided computer programming assistance. Retired U.S. Congresswoman Carrie P. Meek provided the introduction. Final arrangements were made by Addie Hudson.

This book is a tribute to the memory of Big Mama, my first teacher and nurturer who taught me to prepare myself through discipline, desire and dedication to achieve the purpose that God intended.

PROLOGUE

The search for my African roots began during the spring of 1968 in a graduate class at the University of Michigan. Alex Haley, who gave black genealogical research its long overdue spotlight, was telling the story of his African ancestor Kunta Kinte. Alex had a knack for good storytelling, and he described the journey of his slave ancestors from West Africa through the Middle Passage to America. His lecture kept us at the edge of our seats in his description of the capture and cruel journey of the Africans to the land of their servitude. Although his ancestors had come on a different ship, the journey of my ancestors and for most African Americans was the same. I was excited and curious to find out more about his research and the history of my own family.

After the lecture, a group of us stood around and persuaded him to tell us more. We spent well into the evening hours questioning him about genealogical research. Near the end of the evening, I asked him, "Alex, how would I go about researching the roots of my family ancestry?"

He replied in a soft and gentle manner, "Go and talk to the old folks in your family and collect their story before they pass."

*   *   *

On February 20, 2002, I knelt and prayed on the stone-covered courtyard at Cape Coast Castle in Ghana, West Africa. These castles, which sprang up in the late 1600s along the West African coast had been built by the British to warehouse African captives sold as slaves by African middlemen to European slave traders. Here I was at one of them, praying, reflecting and still searching in the senior years of my life for my ancestral roots.

Situated on the upper deck of the Cape Coast Castle, the cannons stood silently, pointing as ghostly sentries toward the open sea, as if protecting the castle fortress from unwanted intruders. The stones of the inner courtyard on the lower level reminded me of tears – tears that had turned to stone - hovering over the mass graves of slaves buried beneath the surface. The African captives had fought valiantly to keep from being led in chains to the dark dungeons below where they would exit what became known as the "Door of No Return," then onto the waiting ships that would take them to a new land.

My visit to Ghana was at the invitation of the honorable Christine Churcher, minister of state for Basic Secondary and Girl Child Education. She and her friend Nana Kweku Egyir Gyepi III, senior divisional chief of Cape Coast, had asked for my assistance in helping them to build a community college.

I had ended my career of 44 years as a successful educator. During that period, I had built and managed community college campuses in four major American community college districts. This had gained me national and international acclaim and had attracted the attention of the Ghanaian government, which was seeking to establish the community college concept as an educational option for its citizens.

While in Ghana, I was able to finish the search for my African roots. It was a journey I reluctantly had embarked upon after my meeting with Haley in 1968. The reluctance was not because of desire but rather because my plate at that point in my life was filled with many aspirations and responsibilities. I was finishing my doctoral dissertation, married, raising a young family and advancing a career in education. But I also knew that many of the old folks in my family were nearing their seventies and eighties. Genealogical research would require travel and a lot of my time.

I decided to go for it.

*   *   *

It was along the Mississippi River at the Battle of New Orleans when Andrew Jackson defeated the English in 1812 that Louisiana was declared a slave state. This resulted in the selling and leasing of thousands of slaves, including my ancestors.

Mama Caroline: "My grandfather Alfred Gooden (later changed to Gooding) was shipped into Louisiana from the state of Virginia and sold to a man named McDade."

Cousin Safronia Thornton/Gage: "My mother Sarah Thornton was shipped into Louisiana and sold on the slave block on her 17th birthday." She gave the date of January 3 but was not sure of the exact year.

The McDade family came to my attention in my research of census data obtained from the Shreve Memorial Library. Prior to coming to Bossier Parish, Louisiana, the McDade family immigrated to South Carolina and moved into Georgia then to Montgomery County, Alabama. It should be noted that slave owners took their slaves with them as they moved to different states. According to the slave schedule of Bossier Parish and the 1850 and 1860 census, the McDade family consisted of five brothers of Scotch-Irish origin. They were:

James G. McDade (5/31/1807-2/28/1852), who owned 50 slaves

William W. McDade (9/29/1810-3/11/1872), who owned up to four slaves

Alexander Jackson McDade (7/28/1815-7/8/1880 or 1889), who owned 15 slaves

Daniel Turner McDade (9/28/1821-1/5/1876), who owned nine slaves

Neal Franklin McDade (4/28/1829-8/19/1899), who owned six slaves.

Mama Caroline: "Alfred Gooding came into the area with two other men – My father-in-law John Warren and a man named Emmanuel Williams." The story goes, she said, that "they jumped ship along a river, waded through swamps, bayous and backwoods until they were captured."

My story is the story of how slave families were separated and sold to different masters and later reunited after slavery. It is also a story of the challenges of the first, second and third generations after Emancipation. Their short-lived freedom as small, independent farmers ended at the turn of the century. Driven by debts owed to white landowners, the family's land was seized. They were forced off the land and became landless, poor and politically disenfranchised. They became pawns of a new sharecropping system of servitude.

It is the story of Jim Crow, legally imposed segregation, lynching and maiming of black men at the beginning of the 20th century as millions of impoverished black families became part of the first major black migration out of the South. They severed their rural southern roots in search of better opportunities in the urban industrial centers of the West, North and East.

Rural southern black families of the 1930s were close-knit and intact units. Families lived in small, rural farming communities called settlements. Some lived on land inherited from their parents and grandparents who, after Emancipation, saved their meager earnings and purchased farmland. Most families lived as sharecroppers on land owned by whites as well as blacks. While parents worked in the cotton fields, other family members and friends reared the young children.

It was during the early forties that my schooling began in a two-room schoolhouse in rural Minden, Louisiana, where black and white children could not share a schoolyard. Our black teachers taught us, "You're starting out behind, so you study and work hard to be two steps ahead of the game." My family reinforced these values. It provided a driving force to move ahead through study and hard work.

Like the exodus of the Hebrews out of Egypt to the "Promised Land" during the period of World War II, my family, along with millions of other black families, became a part of the second black migration and headed West. But these sojourners would find that the cities of the West, East and North were not the promised land of "milk and honey." Instead, they were met by Northern-style racism in employment, housing, public accommodation and health care. The one glimmer of hope was the open access to public education for those who yearned for learning as a path to upward mobility.

What next unfolds is how I translated the dream of my ancestors into my own reality. It is a story about life. Life is consciousness. It is a human journey in time and space filled with storms, valleys, plateaus and peaks. It is a story of standing on the shoulders of the ancestors who laid the foundation for a people unfolding from the "Door of No Return."

INTRODUCTION

By former U.S. Representative Carrie Meek

As a community educator and administrator, Dr. Roy Phillips has opened many doors for students throughout the country. With this book, he now opens his life – providing an interesting and informative account on the importance and impact of family in developing character and community.

In "Exodus From the Door of No Return: Journey of an American Family," Dr. Phillips puts to rest the flawed but sadly prevalent reasoning of so many black people who claim that "We can't all be Alex Haley." Dr. Phillips' book says, "Oh, yes we can; oh, yes we must."

"Exodus From the Door of No Return: Journey of an American Family" is a book for the people because it is a book about a people – a people who survived slavery and all the many guises of that cruel inhuman institution that followed and continue to this day. So often we think of our early African ancestors in America as nameless, faceless people who cowered under the whip, who produced only a handful of heroes whose names we recite during Black History Month.

We think of them as amorphous figures that shifted like shadows from plantation to plantation, from Klan clutches to jail cells and from

Southern cotton fields to Northern factories, leaving few indelible historical footprints.

But they did leave footprints, they did leave shoulders, they did leave legacy. Dr. Phillips found the role models and heroes in his family, and became one himself.

I met Dr. Phillips as a supervisor when he became the campus vice president at the North Campus of Miami Dade Community College (now Miami-Dade College) where I was associate dean of community education. From the very beginning I admired his vision for community education. Let me tell you that when history is written about this college, his name will be at the top of the list. You can't isolate him by saying he was a black educator. He was an educator for the entire community. And he was a darn good educator.

I have a great deal of respect for him because he is not just a theorist. He makes theories work and makes them practical. There is no one who has a better grasp on community education than Roy Phillips. Many people didn't know about colleges - that they could even go to college. But when he came, he went out and developed an outreach program. He's done the kind of advocacy that most college presidents don't know how to do. He has been a change agent. He's always at the front of new ideas.

In addition to his vision on community education, Dr. Phillip's vision on economic development, particularly in the black community, is ground-breaking and commendable. When he came to Miami he became the fulcrum of economic development. He understands the history, dynamics and structure of the black community.

As I went on to become a state representative, then senator, then U.S. congresswoman, I continued to work with Dr. Phillips. The Liberty City Entrepreneurial Center is just one example of an idea that Dr. Phillips had to use the college as a place to help people who wanted to build or develop a small business. The center could provide technical help and show them how to seek funding. He felt that if we had that center – at that time when Northwest Seventh Avenue was very vibrant - it could sustain that community and keep it going. He felt that education was the key. He really believed it.

He brought that idea to me when I was a state senator. We became a very good team. I was able to bring the resources of state government and city of Miami. We married town with gown.

Dr. Phillips was successful because he brought together leaders, grassroots as well as others, to sit down and think of ways to empower people in the community. He stimulated the college to do that kind of thing. The college was involved in social programs where there were federal dollars, but it wasn't willing to take the risk like he was with the business thing he developed. And he got the approval of the board of trustees to do it.

Dr. Phillips has written about all of the things he has done to help the community. This book provides a unique opportunity for the community to share the experiences in the life of a man who succeeded; of a man who came from modest beginnings to serve as a role model. The history and message in "Exodus From the Door of No Return: Journey of an American Family" are too important for us not to read every page.

Dr. Phillips' work should become a literary blockbuster in the category of education, in the category of genealogy, in the category of sociology, in the category of history, in the category of finding a way where there is no apparent way.

This book is testimony that there is a way.

Collecting the Family History

Left to right: Me, cousin Safronia Thornton (1882-1982), son (Roy Jr.), brother, Andrew

Mrs. Mattie Banks/Green (1886-1986), and relative

Collecting the Family History

Cousin, Pairlee Gooding/Rice (1910-2005)

Cousin Arless Willis/Brown (1912), daughter of Maybelle Brooks/Willis and grandson

CHAPTER ONE

From The Door Of No Return

Here I was in 2002 during the senior years of my life . . . still searching for my ancestral roots in Ghana, West Africa.

My search finally ended in 2005 when a Washington, D.C. – based African Ancestry group tested a sample of my DNA and determined that my paternal and maternal ancestry originated from the Mbute and Mende people in the Central African Republic and Sierra Leone respectively.

*   *   *

My mind wandered back to my visit to the Cape Coast Castle of Ghana, West Africa. I stood on the upper deck among the ageless cannons. They appeared to be watching silently as ghostly sentries overlooking the open sea. The castles were first built by the Portuguese as far back as 1471 to achieve three major purposes: To explore the sea route to India and the Far East; secondly, to protect European traders from each other and from the peoples within the region in the competitive trade of goods and people; but most importantly to warehouse African slaves for shipment to the Americas and Caribbean Islands.

Tears rolled down my cheeks as my mind flashed back to the small villages of the bush country of Sierra Leone. Similar incidents also occurred in other parts of the African Gold Coast.

It was during the long period of the slave trade that Akwasi and his sister Abena lived within a small clan with their family. For their livelihood, the family raised goats and grew groundnuts, cassava and yams.

Akwasi and the boys of his age had completed their rite of passage to manhood, while his sister and girls of the village worked with his mother and other women of the village harvesting the crops to be sold in the market place.

During the night of the new moon after the wild dogs and night creatures of the bush ceased their calling, the village was invaded by a group of African slave traders carrying European firearms. The strong men of the village were seized, placed into chains and shackles. Those who resisted were killed. The thatched mud huts were set on fire. The young men and women were captured and prepared for the long trek to the coastal castles.

Abena and the women cried out to their god and spirit of the clan . . . "Ngewo, Nga-fa, save us!" but to no avail. They were swiftly taken into the darkness of the night.

By sunrise of the next day, the band of captives and their captors were deep into the bush country. At midday, the scorching heat of the sun weakened many of them, causing the weaker ones to fall by the wayside . . . falling prey to the wild animals of the bush country.

During the fourth night of the journey, Akwasi gazed into the night sky. He thought of his family left behind and wept bitterly, not knowing his future fate. The night sky appeared before him. Three stars, forming what appeared to be a belt, caught his attention. He remembered the story of the village griot that the three stars had led the early migration of the Mende people from the region of the Sudan many years ago.

The morning of the seventh day, the group arrived at a large stone building overlooking a vast body of water, so vast that he could not see its end. The captives were met by a strange-looking group of men without color in their skin. They spoke an unknown dialect. Akwasi became annoyed and angry at the uninvited search of his body by the strange men.

The inner courtyard appeared to be a marketplace. The African captives were exchanged to European traders by African middlemen for firearms, clothing, beads, rum and other trinkets. When the sale ended, this was the last time Akwasi saw his sister Abena and the women of the village. The women were taken to underground structures on the opposite side of the castle. He was placed with men from other tribal groups. Although they were the same color, Akwasi could not understand their language.

On one side of the courtyard, above the area where the women were placed, there were wooden structures overlooking the courtyard where the pale European traders resided. On the opposite side there was a wooden structure with a cross situated above the labyrinthine dungeons that extended deep underneath the building structures surrounding the castle.

A bearded colorless man dressed in black clothing stood near the opening of the main dungeon entrance. He was waving a thick black book in one hand, as if signaling some strange spirit away as Akwasi and the men were led in chains into the dark dungeons.

Night and day appeared to merge into each other within the dark musty-smelling dungeons where the men lay in chains. It was like a nightmare. The hardness of the stone floor, covered by a layer of straw, placed imprints upon the bodies of the men. The wait appeared to be endless. Each day, more men were added until the cell was filled. Cries and groans from the men echoed throughout the dungeons.

Ghostly figures appeared before Akwasi. He whispered in the darkness . . . "Is this real or is it a dream of my imagination?" The filth and stench of urine and feces caused him to become weak and ill. Food and water were lowered into the dungeons from holes in the upper walls. He refused to eat the strange food.

Those who were too weak to feed themselves were removed to another cell of the dungeons to die. The corpses of those who did not survive the ordeal were removed and placed in mass graves. Others were tossed over the castle wall and swallowed up by the sea.

Occasionally the men were led above for washing and fresh air. Sounds of village songs refreshed his mind. They were songs of weddings, feast and death. They later faded away in the long wait of the deep abyss.

Screams and moans of the women could be heard from across the courtyard as their captors took sexual liberties with them. Offsprings of these illicit relationships were sold to become domestics in the motherland of the phantom slave traders.

At the beginning of the sixth week the captives were led across the courtyard to a large, black door leading from the castle to the beaches below where the boats were waiting to take them out to the ships anchored in the open sea.

New names were given to the departing ancestors because their real names were lost in the ship logs of the departing ships.

I returned as a "son of the diaspora" to tell the story of those who existed the "Door of No Return."

Slavery in Africa

Cannons protecting the slave castle

Me, praying in the courtyards. "The Door of No Return" in the background

Cape Coast slave castle in Ghana, West Africa, built by British in 1665

Slavery in Africa

Me, standing in the courtyards in front of the doors
leading to the slave dungeon in Cape Coast, Ghana

Left to right: Chief Nana Kweku
Gyepi; Elaine Black, Executive
Director of *Tools for Change*
in Miami, Florida; Me,

Left to right: Elaine Black, Me, School Children at Cape Coast Slave Castle

6

CHAPTER TWO

To Be Sold And Let

When my ancestors arrived in America, the oral history of the family and Census records placed them on plantations in the states of Virginia, Maryland, South Carolina, Georgia and Missouri.

On the paternal side of the family, cousin Levada Rice Mitchell provided information from the Rice family archives for the years 1870-1910. The information traces the cruel separation during slavery of the Rice and Harris families within the states of South Carolina and Georgia.

The two families trace their origin to Peter Rice, who was born a slave during the first half of the 1800s in Georgia. He met his wife Katie, a mulatto, on his master's plantation in South Carolina. They had many children, but, unfortunately, they were not all sold as an entire family. All children old enough to be separated from their mother were left behind and sold to a plantation in Georgia.

Great Grandfather Green Harris was one of the children separated from his mother and sold into Georgia while other members of his family, including his half brother Levi Rice, born in 1863, were sold to the Rice Plantation in Claiborne Parish, Louisiana. After Emancipation, Green Harris and other members of the family walked behind a wagon train into Claiborne Parish where they joined the other half of the family.

The oral history of the maternal side of the family illustrates a similar story. The events that followed would begin the definitive recording of my maternal family roots in America and, as with most blacks in the United States, that history is characterized by profound anguish and suffering.

* * *

Rumors spread quickly among the slaves in Brunswick County, Virginia, that some of them would be sold to plantation owners in the new slave states.

The auction sign read:

TO BE SOLD & LET
BY PUBLIC AUCTION
<u>UNDER THE TREE IN THE PUBLIC SQUARE</u>

FOR SALE

The Six Following Slaves:

Emmanuel, About 18 Years Old, An Excellent Laborer Of Good Character

Alfred, About 14 Years Old, Laborer

Nancy, About 20 Years Old, An Excellent Servant And Nurse

Sampson, About 27 Years Old, A Good House Servant

Eliza, About 20 Years Old, An Excellent Washer Woman

Sarah, About 14 Years Old, House Servant

The men belonging to "Leech" estates and the women to Mrs. D. Smit

----

TO BE LET,

on the usual condition of the hirer finding them in food,
clothing and medical attendance,
The Following Male And Female Slaves Of Good Character

Hannibal, About 30 Years Old, An Excellent Servant

Clara, About 35 Years Old, A Laborer

Fanny, An Excellent House Servant And Nurse

ALSO FOR SALE AT ELEVEN O'CLOCK

Corn, Grain, Paddy Books, Muslins, Needles, Pins, Ribbons,
8c-8c

At One O'clock, That Celebrated English Horse Blucher

Word had reached Alfred Gooding's mother that he was to be sold
with five others to plantation owners in the Deep South, where slaves
were in high demand to harvest crops. During the late evening, after
returning from loading the tobacco harvest on wagons heading for
the market place, she wept bitterly. Friends and other relatives from
the nearby huts gathered to offer the family comfort through prayer
and song.

"Uncle Gage," an elderly friend from the group, was called upon
to lead the group in prayer with a song of hope encouraging Alfred

and the others to be strong, have hope and faith and look to God for deliverance.

The night before his departure, Alfred had no desire to sleep. His mother came to comfort him late in the night and flickered out the lamp near his bed. Darkness crept over the room of the little hut of unhewn logs plastered with mud to close the crevices between the logs. Pictures of his childhood appeared before him. As a child, he was allowed to wander and chase the many varieties of chickens, turkeys, ducks and geese in the yard of the big white house where Massa and his family lived. He was now considered a man in the eyes of his Massa, with fully assigned responsibilities of joining the labor gang in the fields of the plantation.

He would miss going up to the big white house with his mother and granny to receive their monthly ration of used clothing, a sack of meal, flour and a slab of bacon. They were allowed to eat from the small garden plot and to eat the chickens that were raised behind the small hut.

Slave mothers had little time for their own children. They had to rise before sunrise with the sounding of the conch horn and line up for the morning meal. To be late would bring lashes from the overseer's whip. The food would be prepared in large quantities by the older women of the plantation. To receive their morning meal, the children would line up and squat along the long, wooden troughs and be fed a morning meal of cornmeal mush. The feeding was similar to the feeding of the livestock of the plantation.

Alfred never knew his father since he had been sold while he was still an infant. Yet he believed that one day he would be free. As the morning hours approached, Alfred's thoughts about his future caused him great anxiety. What would happen to him? Would he be sold to a cruel Massa? Even though he and his mother would see the same moon, they would never see each other again.

The sound of cocks crowing their morning calls drowned out the sound of the wagon wheels slowly approaching the small huts. His mother had risen early and slipped away silently for fear of breaking down upon the departure of her son. She could not bear what she perceived as another death of a family member. Tears rolled down the cheeks of loved ones as departing family members finally loaded into the wagon. Alfred broke down in a loud cry, knowing that he would never see his mother, grandmother, relatives and friends again.

Alfred's grandmother ran behind the loaded wagon with outstretched arms, shouting in despair, uttering over and over again, "de Lawd will be wid you." She fell to her knees weeping bitterly as the wagon disappeared from her view.

Alfred felt an emptiness in his stomach when the wagon stopped with a command of "whoa, whoa," by the driver with a whip in his hand. The slaves were unloaded and placed in a fenced-in area near the public town square. A crowd of well-dressed white men and women gathered to witness and participate in the public auction. A group of white men dressed in black, wearing ten-gallon hats and boots, sat near a raised platform. Another white man, similarly dressed, situated himself behind a podium upon which he placed an open book, a quill and gavel.

He banged his gavel on the podium and spat out a wad of tobacco. He began to chatter fast-sounding words.

"Let the auction begin. This strong, young, black buck would make a fine field hand," the auctioneer shouted, pointing his gavel in the direction of Alfred Gooding. Alfred froze stiff. He began to perspire from fear, anxiety and anger at a system that prized him at the level of the horses and other animals to be sold.

"One hundred and fifty dollars...," the auctioneer shouted out with a smirky smile on his face.

"Two hundred," someone shouted from the crowd. "Two hundred and fifty," another shouted out from the rear.

"Can I hear three hundred dollars," the auctioneer responded. Another shouted out "three hundred and fifty dollars!"

A tall, thin man in black raised his hand and offered... "four hundred dollars."

After a brief silence, the auctioneer hit his gavel upon the podium........"Sold!"

The buyer was part of a slave trading syndicate from South Carolina that transported some of his slaves into the Memphis slave market by rail, where they were joined with other slaves and shipped down the Mississippi River to the port of New Orleans. He shipped the others from Portsmouth, Virginia, also to New Orleans.

Among the latter, Alfred and his companions were marched in line a few hundred yards away to a ship waiting at the dock. They were directed by a lean, red-faced white man dressed in boots, dungarees and a large ten-gallon hat. He carried a pistol in his holster and a rifle in his right hand.

Another white man, with a large potbelly hanging over his belt, stood near the plank of the ship. Several hundred slaves were loaded into the dark hole of the ship. Emmanuel and Alfred sat silently side by side. They had known each other since childhood. Emmanuel had been reared by an older woman on the plantation. His parents had been sold during his childhood.

Thoughts ran through Alfred's mind of his grandmother and mother. He pictured them lighting a fire in the hearth in the front yard. It was the place where they placed flour dough in a big black skillet to prepare his favorite meal of "ho cakes." His grandmother had slipped him a few to take in his small sack, which he opened now for a snack.

The ship had traveled a long distance from mid-afternoon into the late evening. The smell of the sea air drifted down the steps into the dark hull of the ship. They found a pile of empty feed sacks in which they wrapped themselves and fell into a deep sleep.

The next morning, breakfast was a few pieces of ash bread and slices of salt pork. Afterward, they were placed on work detail scrubbing the deck. They also assisted in making minor repairs to the sails of the ship that had traveled thousands of miles hauling slave cargo.

At the end of the fifth day, they entered the port of Charleston, South Carolina, where more slaves were loaded for the long trip to the port of New Orleans.

After a long period of sailing, they finally reached New Orleans, where they were unloaded in an area called "Girt Town." The slaves were marched in line to a destination near the middle of the town. There was a large stockade with many slaves fenced behind barbed wire waiting to be shipped up the Mississippi and Red rivers to a cotton plantation in northwestern Louisiana.

Alfred and Emmanuel could hear the auctioneer rattling off... "One hundred! One-fifty! Can I hear two hundred?" This went on and on into the evening until the last slave was sold. There were hundreds of slaves - men, women and children dressed in shabby clothing - with small bundles of belongings, their only possessions. Some were chained in leg irons. These were the ones who had a long runaway history.

Before being loaded onto a steam ship, the slaves were fed in shifts in long wooden troughs that were filled with food by groups of slaves who had been trained to provide large servings.

The men, women and children were packed into the ship. Alfred and Emmanuel were befriended by a man named John Warren, born in 1841 in the state of Missouri. They learned that his parents had been slaves in Kentucky and sold into Missouri to a plantation owner. Warren was a medium-sized, brown-skinned man with black curly hair. He spoke English well and appeared to be well-bred. He said that his master was selling away his slaves. Slave owners in Missouri had heard that the Civil War was coming to a close and the president was soon to issue an edict for their freedom.

The ship pulled away from the dock during the late evening and headed north to a destination where some of the slaves were to be unloaded to work on plantations in the Red River area while others were to be shipped into Vicksburg, Mississippi. The overseers situated themselves throughout the ship to guard the slave cargo.

The odor from the slaves filled the steamboat. Unsanitary conditions persisted from the stench of children and adults releasing their bowels in sections of the boat. The darkness of night spread like a thin curtain over the swift moving current of the mighty Mississippi.

Near midnight, the sky darkened with swift moving clouds, quick flashes of lightning zigzagging across the night sky followed by the rumbling of sharp sounds of thunder. A serious storm was raging before them. Alfred and his companions had witnessed storms before but not of this magnitude and violence. The ship began to rock from side to side. The waves dashed against the ship and caused it to drift off its course. Suddenly, it drifted into a sandbar near the point where the river meandered. The torrential rain began to flood the hull of the ship, which was not adequate for the stormy task.

Pleas for relief came from the slaves and sounded into the night. "Lawd, Lawd, ham mercy on us," the cries sounded out. There was no relief. Alfred and his companions reached out to women who held tightly to their children to shield them from the torrential rain. The captain sounded a distress call. There was a hurried scramble among the slaves to free themselves from chains and leg irons, but there was no one to free them. The overseers were busily engaged, assisting those whom they could help. They were making an attempt to save their valuable cargo.

In the wildness of the melee, Alfred, Emmanuel and John viewed this as an act of God to jump ship and flee for their freedom. They jumped overboard, waded into the shallow water and crawled into the underbrush near the river embankment.

They had arisen from the fury of the storm-driven waters and now had become fugitives. The threesome knew that they had to make haste to distance themselves from the crippled slave ship. Luckily the overseers had no dogs to track them down.

The three men ran well into the night, stopping only a few moments to catch their breath. By morning, they had reached a heavily wooded area of tall yellow pines, oaks and maples. Their clothing and bodies were drenched with water. As they rested on the fallen leaves of the forest, they made a desperate plea to God to protect them.

They entered the swamp and bayou country, gathering wild berries, grapes and small game for food as they prepared to move on. They had no idea of their whereabouts. Early the next morning, they saw rising smoke from a distance. Had they stumbled upon a settlement of 'po-white-folks' living as trappers in the deep forest? Or had they entered a camp of white bounty hunters in search of runaway slaves? These thoughts ran through their mind as they came near the site of the rising smoke.

"John, you go out and see what is 'head o' us, cause you de oldes' one," Emmanuel said. Alfred shook his head in agreement. John crawled through the thick underbrush on his belly and made his way to the edge of the cleared site. He saw small huts and long shotgun-looking houses similar to ones in his native state. He spotted a group of reddish brown men and women with long black hair. To his surprise, he saw men and women who looked like him and his companions.

He crawled back and reported what he had seen. Alfred whispered, "I heard of small villages of runaway slaves and injuns in de mountains of Virginia." They decided to make themselves known.

They approached a tall man clothed in animal skins. He was accompanied by a group of older men, appearing to be the village elders. In a friendly gesture, the village leader raised his hand to signal a welcome to Alfred and his companions. Other members of the small village, including black ones like them, came out to greet them, identifying themselves as former slaves who had found refuge among their Native American friends. The three men breathed a sigh of relief.

A group of women gathered around a large, black kettle-like pot in the middle of a large yard, which was surrounded by the small huts. They used large wooden ladles to stir what appeared to be a corn-like mush. The smell of the food was very appetizing. Portions of smoked boar and deer meat were brought out by the men of the village. The women served delicious, tasty hominy.

During the late evening around a camp fire, villagers joined their new friends who shared stories of their escape from the crippled slave ship.

The village storyteller related stories of the past. A group of drummers and dancers performed a ritual ceremony to commemorate the heritage of the two groups. Alfred had heard his grandmother say that the African drums were forbidden by the Massa for fear of sending messages of a slave insurrection. The elder storyteller of the village shared the story of the village people.

After a few days of lingering in the small village, the three slave fugitives gathered food and their belongings and decided to continue on their journey. Their plans were to travel northward toward the North Star. They were encouraged to follow the route of the bayous and great forest to stay out of the sight of slave bounty hunters.

Their journey took them through thorny bushes, twisted vines and fallen leaves of the great forest. During the night, they gazed at the stars, appearing to rotate on the great sky canopy. The sound of the night creatures and screaming of wild panthers and other varmints kept them alert and focused.

Early one morning after two days of travel, they heard the sound of barking dogs, which had caught their scent. As they drew near, the dogs detected their movement and three of the lead dogs dashed toward them. A desperate attempt was made to fight them away with tree limbs that had fallen from the trees.

The dogs surrounded them as four white men appeared on horse back with rifles cocked and ready to fire at any false movement by the three fugitives. The leader commanded that they recline on the ground on their bellies with hands folded behind their heads. The leader asked in a stern voice, "Who is yo' masters and what plantation did you escape from?"

John replied, "We wuz sold to a man named McDade." The white men knew exactly the location of the plantation along the Red River in Bossier Parish.

The wrists of the three fugitives were bound and they were instructed to walk between the four bounty hunters as they proceeded to the main road where a group of wagons was waiting to take them to the plantation.

Upon reaching the McDade plantation, Alfred and his companions noticed that the area covered several hundred acres with many more slaves than on their former plantation. The majority were field workers. Others were house servants, black smiths, carpenters and coopers. The plantation specialized in the raising of cotton, some sugar cane, peanuts and other row crops.

Many slave huts with small garden plots were situated throughout the large plantation. A stately mansion stood strategically with a beautiful view of the Red River.

After the harvest season, many of the slaves were hired out to work in the large timber industry that was bustling in the area. Others were hired out to work on roads and labor construction jobs in the small towns. This often caused hostility between the slaves and the po' white class who considered this an infringement upon jobs that they occupied.

One day during the late fall, Alfred was walking through the cotton fields that had been stripped bare of their soft white contents.

The stalks were being plowed under to enrich the soil for the next planting season. He was attracted to a petite, brown-skinned girl with long, black hair. She was sitting on a stump, alone, gazing into the sky with one hand shading her eyes. He approached her and asked, "L'il girl, what is yo' name?" She looked up and said shyly, "My name is Frances Brooks." Without hesitation, he replied, "L'il girl, I is gwine to marry you some day." He went about his way and left her sitting there.

Frances Brooks was being trained as a house servant and nurse maid. She was born in 1853 in the state of Louisiana. Her parents, Green and Lear Brooks, were born in 1827 and 1835 respectively, in the state of Maryland, and apparently served as house servants during slavery. The Brooks family appears to have been the product of mixed African and European ancestry, which was always kept silent in the family. They appeared to have been a highly respected and industrious family. The Brooks had seven children. Frances and her brother Benjamin were the only ones born into slavery.

Being a house servant was no guarantee against the brutality of floggings and ill treatment by the Massa and Missus of the house. In fact, one day Frances was given a whipping for an act that was not too pleasing to her Missus.

Alfred was assigned to live with an older female slave named Maud Banks who was born in Virginia in 1820. She served as a surrogate mother and grandmother until he grew to manhood.

In the mid 1860s, rumors spread like wildfire on the McDade Plantation that President Abraham Lincoln had issued a proclamation setting all the slaves free.

Alfred and his slave peers heard of the surrender as they were planting the spring crops. Although the slaves were freed, they were forced to wait until after spring planting.

On the 19th of June, 1865, the slaves of the McDade Plantation gathered near the small wooden huts. Jubilation filled the air. There was shouting, dancing and singing. They sang and feasted into the night, praising and thanking God for their deliverance. Slavery for the family had ended.

Massa McDade made a desperate plea for the slaves to remain on the plantation as hired laborers. He announced that he would provide a parcel of land to slave families who wanted to remain as tenant farmers. Some remained on the plantation until they had earned enough money to purchase their own farm land. The slaves had mastered the skill of farming since this was the only livelihood that they knew.

First-generation families began to farm. Some slave families were already intact, especially those of the house servant class. On the other hand, many of the field slaves yearned to own their own land.

Thousands of black families were displaced by the abolishment of slavery and the dissolution of the plantation system. Among those families were members of the Harris family on my father's side who had been separated from the Rice family members. The Harris faction had been sold to a plantation owner in Georgia while other members of the family were sold to the Rice plantation in Claiborne Parish, Louisiana.

The spirit of the two families was lifted when they received assistance from the newly created U.S. Bureau of Refugees, Freedmen and Abandoned Lands, which had been created by an act of Congress in 1866 to provide aid to newly freed blacks.

Grandfather Ellis Harris: "My father George (Green) Harris was walked as a child behind a wagon train and rode part of the way from the state of Georgia to join with members of his family in Claiborne Parish, Louisiana. He referred to Georgia as the old country."

Displaced slave families were allowed to travel with mule-driven wagon trains bossed by wagon masters who were hired by the Freedmen's Bureau to relocate families separated during slavery.

The wagon trains followed the route of military trails built by both Union and Confederate troops during the Civil War. The trails crisscrossed the Atlantic seaboard states across Georgia, Alabama and Mississippi into Louisiana.

The two families first settled near Homer in Claiborne Parish. They joined with other families and began sharecropping until they earned enough money to purchase their own farm land.

They next moved into the rich farm land of the newly created Webster Parish, also in northwestern Louisiana. The area of settlement became known as Growing Valley because of its rich farm land, running brooks, bayous and rolling hills and red clay-like soil.

Alfred married the li'l girl, Frances Brooks. John Warren married Emma Harris, born 1854 in Homer of Claiborne Parish, Louisiana. Emma is said to have originated from Native and African-American ancestry. Elijah Brooks, the brother of Frances Brooks, married Ruthann Warren, the eldest daughter of John Warren.

Children of the first generation after slavery were born in the late 1860s. The only children to be born to Alfred and Frances were my great grandmother, Amanda, born in 1867, and her brother George, born in 1873.

During the latter part of the 1880s and early 1900s, some of the slave families had earned and saved enough money to buy their own farms. In fact, on April 7, 1887, Alfred and Frances purchased 80 acres of land from the Vicksburg/Shreveport and Pacific Railroad Company for a price of $160. They paid $53.30 plus 7 percent interest each year until the note was paid.

Great Uncle Wil Thornton and his wife Mattie Hamilton purchased 80 acres of land on December 8, 1919, for a cash sum of $400 from F.H. Drake.

The brothers and sisters of Frances Brooks/Gooding purchased small farms: Benjamin Brooks, born 1860, acquired 240 acres; Elijah Brooks, born 1864, acquired 80 acres; Maybelle Brooks/Willis, born in 1885, acquired 80 acres and Chris Brooks, born 1881, acquired 80 acres.

On my paternal side, Great Uncle Levi Rice and his wife Annie Willis/Rice, born in1872, purchased land from two white landowners in 1903. Two hundred acres were purchased from F.H. Drake Sr. and 160 acres from Thomas Creighton Sr. Great Grandfather Green Harris, born in the 1860s, and his wife Hattie Walker/Harris, born in the 1870s, purchased 100 acres alongside his half brother Levi Rice.

Great Grandfather Hardy Waller, born in 1830 in North Carolina, and his wife Amanda Crownover/Wiley/Waller, a mulatto born in 1858 in Louisiana, acquired 80 acres.

Other enterprising black families purchased farm land in the Growing Valley community. They included Edmon Banks, who owned 300 acres in the Couchwood farm area.

The post-slavery families were enterprising. They knew that their future in America was tied to the land as small farmers. However, the political and economic future of black families in the Deep South began to turn sour as the 19th century came to an end. The first and second generations began to face major challenges as the storms of legal segregation, discrimination and blatant racism loomed above the horizon of the new century.

Ancestors of the Slavery and Reconstruction Generation

**Aunt Alice Lowery
Community Midwife
(1851-1960)**

**Maternal Great-Grandfather
Shepherd Lee (1869-1950s)**

**Paternal Grandmother
Amanda Crownover/Wiley/
Waller (1858-1941) and son,
Andrew Waller (1882-1942)**

**Maternal Grandmother Sarah
Chatman/Cook/Wilson (1863-1958)**

Maternal Grandfather James
Warren (1876-1916)

Paternal Great-Grandfather Green
Harris and Great-Grandmother
Hattie Walker/Harris (1860s)

Uncle Levi Rice (1863-1941) and wife Annie Willis/Rice (1872-1937)

CHAPTER THREE

Freedom Turns Sour

The short-lived period of Reconstruction was coming rapidly to a close even before the first post-slavery generation had grown into adulthood. Despite some seemingly political and economic advances for blacks, including the 40-acres-and-a-mule provisions and a few Congressional seats held by blacks during the period, the southern white aristocracy soon regained control of the South and its newly freed slaves. Unable to gain market access for their farm products or obtain capital for investment in required farm machinery, black farmers became indebted to and dependent on white landowners in a crippling and demeaning system called sharecropping.

Led by the Ku Klux Klan, white vigilante terrorist groups spread a reign of terror - burning, lynching and maiming of black men - throughout the South and parts of the North. Southern states enacted Jim Crow laws, placing restrictions upon black citizenship and voting rights, education and public accommodation. Poll taxes and literacy tests were imposed to prohibit blacks from voting and jury participation.

* * *

Despite the economic hardships, black families in the South learned how to survive, and in the midst of misery, people managed to fall in love and marry. In the 1880s, Amanda Gooding, Alfred and Frances Brooks/Gooding's eldest child and only daughter, married Shepherd Lee.

Born in 1869 in Louisiana, "Shep" Lee was the son of Eli Lee and Luvenia Thornton/Lee, a native of Georgia. As a child, I remember Grandpa Shep, a slender man standing 6'5", who carried an ax on his shoulders to cut timber in the back woods. As a part- time minister, he loved the spirituals.

Although a spiritual leader, Grandpa Shep had a reputation of being tough. Once he and a man named John Dudley got into a dispute. To settle their differences, they agreed to a gun duel. The day of the duel, each man walked his distance, turned and fired at each other. The pellets of Grandpa's shot gun ricocheted off a fence rail, ripping off one of Dudley's fingers. Following that incident, no one else ever challenged Grandpa to another duel.

After Alfred Gooding died, Shep and Amanda Lee took on the care of Gooding's widow - Amanda's mother - Frances. Like so many other blacks in the South, my great grandparents were sharecroppers. Family members, who also cut logs in the rich yellow pine lumbering industry of northern Louisiana and worked in the expanding rail industry, had been unable to pay off debts a white landowner claimed was due to him. At issue were 80 acres of land that Alfred Gooding had purchased in 1887 from the Vicksburg Shreveport Pacific Railroad Company.

"A mean white man by the name of Hudson forced them from the land, causing them to become landless," remembered my grandmother Caroline, the eldest daughter of the Lees' 10 children.

Born June 19, 1882, Mama Caroline grew into a tall, slender, beautiful woman. During her teen years, she assisted her father and mother in sharecropping, vowing that one day she would own her own farm. Like the black women of her time, she learned to plow, chop and pick cotton, ride a horse, hitch and drive a mule team like a man. She was tough like her father.

Life for Mama Caroline and other black families in Growing Valley centered on the Missionary Baptist Church, the primary church of the black South. By custom, a church and a school would be erected on the same site. The two institutions became the religious, educational and social center of the community.

In accordance with church records, Daniel James called a small group of people together to form a church on the old McDonald place in 1884. The first Growing Valley Missionary Baptist Church was beneath a bush in Elijah Brooks' back yard. The church later relocated to an old cotton house on Gasson Brooks' place, then later to Blake Hill. The first church house was made from rough-cut lumber purchased from the Jodie Battle sawmill. Ministers who could read and write were pastors, including the Rev. Jeffie Terrell, who was pastor for the first seven years.

A line of other ministers followed, some of them educators who served as principals of the newly organized Growing Valley Elementary School for Colored Children. The Rev. B. D. Lee, my father's first teacher, served as pastor and principal of the school in 1926. Beginning in September 1930, the Rev. Jessie Hodge Dixon, an educator who eventually obtained a doctorate in theology, served as pastor for 60 years until his death in 1990.

The historic mainstream of Growing Valley Missionary Baptist Church created a bond between family, church and school. It provided the foundation for religious and social development. It also played a significant role in preserving the history of the people. Church records recorded the births, baptisms, marriages and deaths of its parishioners. My cousin Steve Fullwood, served as church clerk in 1900. He was followed by Uncle S.J. Waller.

The local lay board of the church resided in a Board of Deacons, selected from outstanding Christian men within the church community. Many of these men associated themselves with other fraternal associations, including the Fraternal Order of the Prince Hall Masons. Great Grandfather, John Warren was one of the first organizing deacons.

The church also served as the first school. The early teachers were Cousin Bessie Lowrey/Johnson, granddaughter of Aunt Alice Lowrey, the community midwife; cousin Evelyn Banks/Gooding, who married Green Gooding, son of George Gooding. Luvenia Gage, sister to Uncle Richard Gage, my early childhood nurturer, taught at the Valley Spring and St. James church, organized in 1866. These early teachers were highly devoted to the teaching of colored children. They would rise in the early morning hours and walk approximately 10 miles each day to teach in these rural schools.

The Growing Valley Elementary School for colored children was erected on the same site of the Growing Valley Missionary Baptist Church in the early 1900s. The Rev. Jonah Parker, who served as principal from 1935-1939, said the school was erected with funds from the Julius Rosenwald fund. Rosenwald was a wealthy Jewish philanthropist who served as chairman of Sears & Roebuck. His foundation provided funds to aid the cause of Negro education in rural areas of the South. The organizing trustees for the school were: Uncle Oliver Walker, who could not read or write but was a great supporter of education, and Uncle George Gooding, who was well-read for this period in our history. They later were joined by Uncle S.J. Waller, Cousin Wesley Brooks and J.D. Hudson as trustees.

Upon reaching adulthood, Mama Caroline, who represented the second generation after slavery, married James Warren, the son of John and Emma Warren. Born in 1876 in Growing Valley, Louisiana, James Warren, like his father, was an achiever and independent minded. He shunned indebtedness to white men for fear of land seizure for unpaid debt.

After marriage, the young couple moved to Natchitoches, Louisiana, in the early 1900s to tenant farm with the intent of earning and saving enough money to purchase their own farm. When the economy worsened, they returned to the Growing Valley farming community where they began to raise a family, the third generation after slavery.

Their first child of live birth was Mary Jane Warren, my mother, born March 28, 1915. Grandpa James died, probably of heart failure, at a young age, leaving Mama Caroline with three children to rear, my mother, Uncle Dan and Aunt Ruthann.

Mama Caroline remarried to a hometown young man named Will Green. Six children were born to this marriage. The family sharecropped until it had enough money to buy a small farm.

But the family's hard-working days were not without racial strife. Near the end of summer in 1928, Tom Brooks, the son of Uncle Chris Brooks, was lynched by an angry mob of white men outside the town of Minden, Louisiana.

Tom Brooks was a brash young man who did not compromise his principles to accommodate the racism of arrogant white men, an attitude not prevalent among black men at that time. Some white men considered black men with this type of attitude as crazy, and they feared them with a passion. The only way to deal with this type of black man, they reasoned, was to lynch him as an example to other black men of his type.

Cousin Arless Brown/Willis remembers Tom walking through a predominantly white community. He was confronted by a group of men and accused of "staring too hard at a white woman's underwear," which was hanging from a clothesline in the yard.

For this alleged act, the mob assaulted him by tying his feet with a rope and dragging his body behind an automobile until his death. They hung his body from a tree to display as a lesson to other black men.

Uncle Chris and other men from the community came to claim Tom's body but were refused. The body hang until birds of prey came to pick its flesh. This was the racial climate in many towns of the Deep South during the period of the 1920s and 30s. Black women feared for the lives of their husbands and sons. This fear was passed on to future generations.

The responsibility for rearing and nurturing children became the responsibility of the entire community. My mother Mary Jane had now grown into a teenager and soon attracted the eyes of boys in the community. She had dropped out of school to help her mother and father as her mother had during an earlier period.

She met my father, John Phillips, nicknamed Bill, at school and church.

Dad was born an illegitimate child on September 9, 1909. Abandoned by his mother, Eliza Harper/Lee, who had four other children, he was placed in the hands of Hardy and Amanda Waller. He was later taken in by Proff and Lula Phillips. In those days, unwanted children were taken in informally by caring families of the community, a practice handed down from slavery during which children were often separated from their real parents. The Phillips had no children of their own, and like many landless black families, they moved about, living and working on farms owned by white and black landowners.

Proff Phillips was of mixed African and European ancestry. He was born in 1865 of parents from the state of Mississippi. Big Mama, Lula Phillips, was born April 4, 1877, in Louisiana as a member of the Hamilton family where there were 11 other children. Her mother was Laura Lowery/Hamilton, born 1862 in Louisiana. Big Mama's father was Tom Hamilton, referred to as "Pink Jemison" because of his light complexion. He was born in 1860.

Big Mama and Proff Phillips dressed their adopted son in the best clothing and taught him to read and write. He was a slender, attractive, bright child who dropped out of school at grade seven to care for his older parents.

He began courting Mary Jane, "Muh" and on December 25, 1932, they were married by the Rev. Jessie Dixon, pastor of the Growing Valley Missionary Baptist Church. On June 19, 1933, they gave birth to their first son, my brother, Andrew James Phillips.

Second Generation After Slavery

Maternal Great Aunt Maybelle Brooks/
Willis, sister to Great-great Grandmother
Frances Brooks-Gooding (1885-1968)

Maternal Grandmother Mama Caroline
Lee/Warren/Green (1882-1984) and
sister Hattie Lee/Dudley (1909 -1970s)

Left to right Great Uncle Willie (Wil) Thornton (1880 1930s), wife Mattie
Hamilton (1880s-1940s) and son Henry (Bay) Thornton (1910-1995)

Religious Institutions Established During the (1880s-1900s)

The Original Growing Valley Missionary
Baptist Church, Organized 1884

The Original Bright Star Missionary
Baptist Church Organized, 1895

Valley Spring Missionary Baptist
Church, Established 1912

CHAPTER FOUR

Life In A Rural Southern Community

Life for black families had changed little since Reconstruction. Children were cared for by grandparents and older adults as the young parents worked the fields as their slave parents had done before them.

During this period, the white majority referred to us as coloreds, Negroes, or niggers, depending upon the circumstances in which we found ourselves. My mother, father, grandparents and relatives started their lives as part of this system of servitude.

* * *

A sound of thunder drowned out the baby's first cry. The late autumn skies quickly blackened as a strong gale blew against a wooden shanty on a red, clay dirt road. Dad remembers that it was nearly three o'clock in the afternoon on November 26, 1934. Muh's birth pains had started near the noon hour and reached their peak in the late afternoon.

The storm increased in its intensity as Aunt Alice Lowery, the community midwife, gave comfort to the young teen mother. Aunt Alice had delivered many babies during her 80 years. She had delivered my brother Andrew a year earlier. Born a slave in the 1850s,

Aunt Alice was still able to get about and perform her midwife duties. She lived to the ripe age of 109.

"Bill," Aunt Alice said in a soft voice, "go and fetch some warm water." Water had been heating in a black kettle on an old iron stove, which was in the small kitchen-bedroom near the back door. Dad, a young man in his early twenties, hurried into the kitchen. He poured warm water from the kettle into a face pan, grabbed a towel from the nearby rack and handed it to Aunt Alice. Muh was pushing hard as Aunt Alice assisted her. The little boy slipped from his mother's womb and took the first breath of air from Mother Earth.

"It's another little baby boy," Dad exclaimed in excitement. "I declare, it looks just like Mae Jane with those deep dimples," Big Mama chimed.

Gently placing the towel around the baby's wet body, Aunt Alice cleaned and placed the baby boy into the arms of his smiling mother. A bolt of lightning brightened the room. The oil lamp flickered as a gush of wind lashed against the shotgun shanty. An old folk's saying had it that the fury of a storm could be lessened by placing an ax in the ground facing the direction of the storm. Grandpa Shep Lee rushed out the back door, grabbed an ax near the pile of freshly cut pinewood. The wind blew sheets of rain against his tall frame, and with all of his might he pointed the ax in the direction of the storm and slammed the blade into the ground. The sound of raindrops echoed from the tin roof top. After he returned, the wind continued to ruffle through the tall yellow pines and oaks that surrounded the little wooden shanty.

Then the storm passed and the towering thunder head clouds moved into the distance. A smell of wet, red clay blew through the house. The little baby boy was carefully dressed and tucked away into a small makeshift dresser drawer used as a temporary bed. As the evening shadows lengthened, a red crowned rooster flapped its wings and flew atop the wooden fence surrounding the small shanty, stretched its neck and cackled. The fall storm had produced a cool breeze and with it my arrival.

The storm would be a menacing metaphor of the magnitude and frequency of storms that would occur in my life. But it would seem that somehow the equivalent of a Grandpa Shep also would be there to lessen the fury.

During the late evening hours after a long work day, Big Mama shared stories of her past, read to us the tales of Mother Goose, Br'er Rabbit and the Fox and the Bear. She used the stories to teach us valuable lessons about growing up in America as black males. She knew that any time during our lifetime we could be lynched as Tom Brooks had for getting out of his "place" with certain white people. She taught us that we always had to be vigilant around certain white folks and play the role of the sly Fox and clever Br'er Rabbit to remain ahead of their game. These stories inspired us to read, write, speak and dream.

"Learn all you can and never let anger or bitterness control your life," she would say. She read to us from Proverbs 15:1: "A soft answer turneth away wrath, but grievous words stir up anger." She also said, "Take each hardship as a challenge to be able to rise above the storms that will face you."

Nighttime was storytelling time. The front porch was the classroom since it was too hot during the long summer months to remain inside before bedtime. The quietness of the summer nights invited the calling of the whippoorwill, singing of the katydid and the croaking of the pond frogs. The canopy of the night sky was covered with the stars of the Milky Way and the summer constellations. Big Mama knew the story of the great constellations: the large and small dippers, the North Star, the dragon, the Triad and many others, including the comets that we referred to as shooting stars. This inspired me to want to learn about science.

She referred to the almanac to forecast the weather and planting of certain crops in the spring. When we became ill, she used old home remedies to bring us back to health.

When Big Mama was away, my brother and I were placed in the care of a dearly beloved member of the community, Richard Gage, whom we referred to as "Uncle Richard". Born in the 1880s, he had no children but had a special caring for us. He was related to the family through a former marriage. He lived near his brother in an old rundown log cabin, probably an old slave hut, with the ground as a floor. Near the front door was an old fireplace used for cooking and heating during winter. The rear of the house sheltered a roosting place for bantam chickens that he reared. During the weekends, Muh and Dad would allow me to visit him. He and Big Mama were my early mentors. I cared for and loved them both.

Early one Saturday morning, we were awakened by a disturbance of the chickens. Uncle Richard reckoned that it was an old coon or hawk that could be frightened away by a loud shout and clapping of our hands. After several shouts and clapping of our hands, the little bantam chickens continued their noisy cackling. Uncle Richard grabbed his double-barreled shotgun from over the fireplace. He cracked opened the front door to obtain a view of the front yard where the chickens were frantically running about. He spotted a huge, black snake that had coiled itself around a limb of the dead tree.

He called out to me by nickname: "Little Joe, come outside near me." He placed the shell into the chamber of the gun. Standing firmly and positioning the butt of the gun against his inner right shoulder, he aimed, squeezed the trigger and fired. The snake fell from the tree with a clump as it hit the ground. It was injured but not dead. He grabbed the snake by its wiggling tail, rotated it in a whirling motion, and with a quick snap, broke its vertebrae. He finished the kill with a second round.

Uncle Richard was part of a tradition and value system tying families, single and older people into a community kinship. Community values and traditions grew out of three major institutions created during Slavery and Reconstruction: family, church and school.

Sunday was a special day. With a day of rest from the hard work of the fields and backwoods, families would dress in their best and load into mule-driven wagons. The sight of families traveling down the main gravel road leading to the church was inspiring. Families loved a chance to socialize and catch up on the gossip for the week. Little girls and boys would giggle and blush. My favorite seat was in the rear of the wagon, where I could swing my feet.

The church bell tolled loudly as we neared the church yard. Uncle Joe, the son of Hardy and Amanda Waller, was the sexton. He rose early to ring the bells, signaling the beginning of Sunday morning worship.

I remember the services. I sat between Muh and Dad in anticipation of the morning worship. The deacons introduced the hymns handed down by our slave ancestors:

"A charge to keep I have
A God to glorify
 Who gave his son my soul to save
And fit it for the sky.
To serve the present age,
My calling to fulfill,
Oh may it all my pow'rs engage
To do my Master's will."

As the deacons would shout out each stanza, the congregation would chime in, raising its voices in a harmonious melody of praises for a gracious God who had brought us through another week. The congregation would respond with "Amen, praise the Lawd," and "Yes, Jesus, my Savior, you been so good to me."

The songs and prayers were a great inspiration and psychological uplift to a people who toiled in the sun-scorched cotton fields for a meager wage that kept them always in debt to the general store.

After church, a delicious, hearty meal was served. The fattest chicken from the yard that had been isolated and especially fed for this occasion was killed. A serving of turnip greens, freshly picked black-eyed peas, potato salad, corn bread, peach cobbler and pound cake topped the menu. This was the time of visits from relatives, friends and the minister. Following the meal, the old folks gathered, shared news and gossiped about recent occurrences within the small community. The children organized games of hide-and-go-seek, "Ring Around the Rosy," "London Bridge" and other games, which occupied our time until evening services.

During this period, there was no separation between church and school, but schools for black children were unequal to schools for white children. The system of segregated education was designed to place in the minds of black children and their parents that they were inferior to whites and that even education would not make them equal to the poorest of white folks.

Growing Valley Elementary School went from grades one through six. Children who were fortunate and had relatives living at Minden could attend there for junior and high school. The Rosenwald-funded school also received limited state support for its operation. Ms. Grace Landry, a local Negro educator, served as a parish supervisor to administer colored schools in Webster Parish.

The politics of Huey Long, a populist governor of Louisiana during the late 1920s, greatly advanced the education of poor white and black children within the state, although resources for black children continued to be inferior to those for whites. Black children were the recipients of secondhand books, school furnishings, equipment and facilities passed down from white public schools. One could discern the number of times a book had been used by the number of names written in the ownership section of the book.

Even though Dad and Muh did not acquire a high school education, they planted a seed of encouragement in the minds of my brother and me to fulfill their dreams in the coming age of America. They, like many young, rural black families were willing to work hard, make personal sacrifices, save their money and place their children as the highest priority in their lives.

From this background, my brother and I were enrolled at Growing Valley Elementary in October 1939 and 1940 respectively. Our first teacher, Cousin Evelyn Banks/Gooding, also had taught Muh and Dad.

Vivid memories remain in my mind regarding my first day in school. I was very upset, having to depart company with Muh and Big Mama, who had allowed me to roam from sunrise to sunset in my secret play areas. My brother and I had to rise early each morning before sunrise to prepare for school, which was five miles away. There was no yellow school bus to take us. We were expected to be at school each day, rain or shine, sleet or snow, before the ringing of the school bell. If done too often, arriving late to school got you a spanking.

Each morning Muh prepared breakfast and lunch. Lunch consisted of two biscuits filled with syrup and two pieces of dry salt fried bacon, carefully placed in a small syrup bucket. The closed lid on the bucket was airtight. The wire handle was secured on the straps of our overalls and carried on our backs. Each morning, we were joined by our uncles and aunt, Mama Caroline's younger children. We walked the long distance along the red clay road to school. Sometimes we would stop and play along the way until a white neighbor told our parents. A good whipping put an end to that affair.

After the first few days, I fell in love with school. Big Mama had taught me the alphabet and how to read. The principal, Professor Jonah Parker, who resided in Minden until 2003, took a liking to me.

During the late fall of my first year in school, a fleet of black Model T Ford automobiles filled with a group of stern-looking white men dressed in black, drove onto the school yard at recess. The men - the sheriff and his deputies - stepped from their automobiles with the highest display of authority. They shouted to the principal to come out of the building in full view of the pupils and teachers. The sheriff said a few words, then handcuffed and placed the principal into one of the cars and drove away.

A hush fell over the children as we were marched back into the school. It was a sight that remains with me until this day. I later learned that the principal had been falsely accused of having sexual relations with one of the female students. From this experience, I developed a deep dislike of white lawmen riding past the house in black automobiles. In fact, one day while playing in the front yard, I angrily shouted out at the sheriff as he drove by. My father quickly rushed to the front yard and restrained me from throwing rocks at the sheriff's automobile. Dad instructed me to never challenge the authority of a white man. Disappointed by my father's instruction, I began to dislike myself as a black child. I began to think that there was something wrong with black skin. Each morning, I washed my face with water and soap, wishing that I could remove my black skin.

As the fall days advanced, the women of the community canned fruits, made winter clothing, quilted bedding and patched up the holes in doors to keep the cold air from entering. Heavy bed linen was essential since there was only one heat source, a fireplace in the living room. Most of the heat from the fireplace was lost through the chimney. The men of the community hunted small game to supplement the food supply. Cutting and hauling timber was the major winter season occupation. It added to the family income.

Late fall also was the season for the slaughtering of farm animals - not a welcome time for children who had become fond of some of them. Muh had nurtured the rearing of a small piglet that came into the house frequently to be cuddled. When it was slaughtered, I shut myself into my room and cried.

The method of slaughtering animals was especially cruel. Dad and the men of the community gathered for this occasion, sharpening their axes and knives to bludgeon the animals. The most common livestock for slaughter was the pig. The sledgehammer was used to hit the pig in the head to kill it. After its death, the body was dipped head first into a barrel of boiling water. After the dip, the animal was hung by its feet and scraped of its body hair. A sharp knife was used to split open its mid-section to remove the organs from the thoracic and abdominal sections. All of the internal organs, including liver, stomach and intestines, would be cleaned, salted and properly stored for cooking. The muscular exterior of the animal would be cut into sections, smoked, salted and stored in the smokehouse in the rear of the small shanty. The prepared meats were placed in sacks and hanged from the smokehouse ceiling with hooks. The meats were shared with widows and older members of the community in need.

During the sugar cane harvest, the men gathered at the mill where the cane stalks were placed in a huge container that allowed the juices to be squeezed out of the stalks. This was accomplished through the rotation of a team of mules that was hitched to the rotating machine, which liberated the cane juices. The sweet juices were poured into a huge, black pot that was preheated to its boiling point. The boiling juices were properly stirred and converted into delicious sorghum syrup, which was poured into gallon buckets for storage in the smoke house. Each family in the community shared in the harvest.

The holiday seasons were special times of family gatherings with relatives and friends. Three special holidays were celebrated: Christmas, Easter and the 19th of June. The Thanksgiving holiday was generally considered the starting period for the preparation of the Christmas holiday season. The preparation of the Christmas holiday also included the New Year holiday. Muh and Big Mama started their baking of special Christmas food near the end of November. They prepared cakes of all flavors, cookies, sweet potato pies, cobblers, and chicken, turkey and ham from the smokehouse. It was fun hanging around the kitchen as Muh's little helper, tasting foods, licking out of pans and enjoying the delicious aroma.

A few weeks before Christmas, Dad and Muh went to town on Saturday and spent the entire day shopping for toys, clothing, fruits and nuts. My first memory of Christmas was the year of 1940, when Santa Claus delivered a tricycle and a little red wagon for my brother and me. There was a special greeting when a person entered your home. The greeting was "Christmas gift," and the response was "Give it here."

By the first of February, people would check their almanacs for weather predictions, indicating the beginning of the spring. The strong March gales signaled the appearance of cirrus clouds followed by rolling cumulus clouds, the beginning of warm weather.

April showers brought the blossoming of wild cherry trees in the nearby bayous and swamps. It was time for planting, and Easter was around the corner. It was the time for the birth of little baby chicks from the fertilized eggs of cackling hens that closely guarded the hatching brood of chicks. It was the time for religious revivals and the calling of sinners to salvation. It was the time for baptisms in the ponds and backwater of the bayous.

People came from all the churches, Baptist, Methodist and the Church of God in Christ, to hear good preaching, testifying, singing and saving of souls. Dad and Muh had formed a group to sing at special occasions.

One Friday evening, Aunt Ruthann, Muh's sister, her husband, Uncle Leamon, and their daughter, Lola Mae, came to the house to practice their quartet singing before the evening service. They rehearsed one of their favorite songs, "Bound for the Promised Land."

> "I am only on a journey
> In this worried troubled land.
> My home is over yonder
> On the bright and shining stand.

Many times I feel discouraged
When my hope is almost gone.
But when Jesus sits beside me,
With the joy bell ringing
And the Savior clinging
I am bound to travel on."

Before they sang the last stanza, I fell fast asleep. They decided to leave me to sleep through the night. The singing revival was held at the Church of God in Christ, located across the cotton field from the house, about a half a mile away. I woke up to find myself alone. The house was pitch dark. I got out of bed and began to search for my brother and parents, but they were nowhere to be found. Maybe they had all gone next door to Big Mama's house, I thought. I unlatched the door and went outside, heading to Big Mama's house. The air was chilled and the moonlight cast my shadow behind me. I knocked on Big Mama's door and there was no answer. A funny feeling ran through my body. I felt my hair standing on my head. I was alone and afraid.

Thoughts ran through my mind that my parents, brother and Big Mama had been taken away by the parish sheriff, like the principal had been taken from the school. Terrified, I let out a loud scream, as loudly as my five-year old voice would allow: "Muh! Muh! Daddy! Daddy!" No one answered. I could hear the echo of my scream resounding from the surrounding woods in the stillness of the night.

After screaming and crying for what appeared to me as about an hour, I saw Dad jump the fence, followed closely by Muh, running toward me in desperation. Dad grabbed me into his arms, hugging me tightly. "Little Joe, baby! Is you all right? We nevva gonna leave you again." I was relieved after being given a glass of buttermilk and tucked away into bed again. I was comforted in knowing that Muh and Dad would never leave me again.

The 19th of June was the colored folks' Fourth of July. It was the day of jubilee set aside for the celebration of freedom from slavery. This event kept alive the memory of the passage of the ancestors from slavery. As families left the rural South, the festival was taken to the urban centers of the nation.

My first memory of the 19th of June was a big picnic Grandpa Shep organized in 1939. The men formed a baseball team while the women prepared lemonade, ice cream and cake. The ice cream was prepared in a hand-driven tub-like cylinder filled with sweetened vanilla flavored milk. The rotating cylinder tub was placed in an ice-packed wooden bucket filled with ice and covered with salt that prevented the ice from melting too quickly. The tub was rotated by hand until the content inside was frozen into a delicious ice cream.

During the period of the late 1930s, small southern towns allowed some blacks to settle there, giving black entrepreneurs a chance to set up shop. Black pioneers led the way. One such pioneer was the Rev. James Green and his wife Mattie, who before her death at the age of 100, revealed her history to me. She was born September 12, 1886, to Edmon and Lucy Banks in Couchwood, Louisiana. I knew Mrs. Green as an enterprising woman. In 1935, she and her husband purchased a lot for $150 in the nearby town of Cullen/Springhill, Louisiana, and built a hotel there. They were the first blacks in the town. A group of white men confronted them and tried to force them out of town but failed.

During the late thirties and forties other black merchants, including Henry Rhone, John Hughes and Booker Tatum, opened grocery, dry goods and barber shops, cafes, auto garages, funeral homes and lumber yards to serve black families moving into town. The small black community patronized black merchants and went uptown to buy merchandise not available, such as clothing, from white merchants.

Cullen/Springhill was as southern as you get. It was the last town going north before reaching the Arkansas border. The area was the center of the timber industry, especially the heavily populated yellow pine forest that produced pulp for paper manufacturing.

The town of Cullen had a small post office and train depot. The town was situated along US 371 where a huge paper mill dominated the area with a tall smokestack that polluted the air with its smelly sulphur dioxides. The black section of town sat off from the main street, where the small white cafes and businesses were located.

Country music blasted from those cafes where blacks entered and were served only from the rear of the shops.

Blacks lived in "Froggy Bottom," named for the abundance of frogs in the surrounding ponds and swamp area. One could sit on the front porch during the late evening and hear the croaking and singing well into the night.

Segregated Education of the 1930s and 1940s

Children and teachers of the Cullen/Springhill Colored Elementary School, 1942

Rev. Jonah Parker (1912-2003), Principal Growing Valley
Colored Elementary/ Junior High School (1930s)

Children and teachers of the Growing Valley Colored Elementary and Junior High School
1939 left to right cousin Evelyn Banks/Gooding, Rev. Jonah Parker

CHAPTER FIVE

Beginning Of The Great War: From Field To Paper Mill

On December 7, 1941, the Japanese dropped bombs on Pearl Harbor, sank American ships and destroyed naval installations. The military attack put America into World War II. The war spurred the need for the nationalization of crucial industries required to build ships, airplanes, tanks, ammunition and other implements of war. Manpower was in high demand.

* * *

The demand for labor caused Dad also to move the family from Growing Valley to Cullen/Springhill. The town was the site of the Southern Craft Paper Mill Manufacturing Company, which employed hundreds of people in the cutting, logging and manufacturing of paper products.

Dad worked at jobs reserved for black men, namely unskilled and hard-labor intensive. Muh hired herself out as a domestic, cleaning, washing and ironing for white folks. My brother and I were left in the care of Big Mama, who also watched the children of other working parents in the community. Big Mama was now widowed from the loss of Grandpa Proff Phillips, who passed on November 3, 1937.

We were the first generation of black children to attend school in the Cullen/Springhill community. The school was located in the

Cullen Missionary Baptist Church. My brother and I enrolled in the elementary school, which offered grades one through six. There were no provisions for black children for grades seven through twelve. Upon completion of the sixth grade, children either dropped out of school to work, or if their parents were fortunate to have relatives living in Minden, approximately 25 miles away, arrangements were made for them to attend school there. Springhill, two miles away from Cullen, provided a comprehensive consolidated school, grades one through twelve, for white children. By law, black children were forbidden to attend schools with whites. Transportation was provided to white children, but no such services were provided for black children at that time.

The school year for black students started in October, after harvest, and closed in April, the beginning of the planting season. The school schedule was intended to ensure the availability of black children to work with their parents in the fields of white land-owners. Just prior to school opening, we would accompany Muh to the fields to pick cotton. We were given a small cotton sack that was pulled down the long, and seemingly endless, rows of cotton. We picked the soft contents from the thorny boles of cotton. I rejoiced each evening to see the setting sun, which meant an end to the day.

Black teachers were selected from those who had reached at least the eleventh grade. Very few black teachers possessed college degrees. Teachers were strict disciplinarians. If you acted up in school, you received a whipping, and word was sent home to your parents who administered a second whipping if the infraction was serious enough. School started and ended each day with religious devotional services, the pledge of allegiance to the flag and the singing of patriotic songs.

The physical conditions in the old church house did not encourage effective teaching and learning. The seats were old wooden benches without any provisions for writing. During the winter season, the building was overheated by an old iron heater located in the front of the church. Tin piping was connected to the iron stove to remove the smoke and much of the heat to the outside of the building. Poor air circulation within the church assembly produced boredom, fatigue and a lack of interest in learning.

Two female teachers, Ms. Ross and Mrs. Walton, divided the children by grade levels. They did the best they could under the circumstances. They attempted to spend time with each group on a rotational basis. While one group was taught, the others would perform an assigned lesson. My lack of attention and playfulness with the girls in the class caused me to repeat the second grade.

The school placed a great deal of attention upon cleanliness, prompting daily physical inspections of each student's teeth, hair, fingernails, ears and eyes. Unkempt physical conditions often resulted in the administration of corporal punishment. Children who came from homes where good hygiene and grooming were not the rule became the butt of jokes by their peers. This often caused some children to drop out of school at an early age.

In addition to schoolwork, chores took up our time after school and on weekends. My brother and I took pride in cutting and stocking wood, feeding the chickens and pigs and running errands for neighbors.

The end of the school year was a time of celebration. The teachers spent many weeks preparing and coaching students to participate in dramatic, musical and oratorical performances. These events provided my brother and me an opportunity to make our parents proud as we excelled in drama and oratory.

The end of the school year also meant returning with Muh to assist her parents on the farm back in Growing Valley. The first part of the planting season consisted of chopping and removing weeds from the germinating corn and cotton seedlings. Working in 100-degree heat was hard work. During the summer months and also on weekends during the school year, I worked in a small grocery store in Cullen owned by Booker and Savanna Tatum. I stocked the shelves, swept the floors and waited on customers at the cash register. The job provided me an opportunity to earn money while learning to become entrepreneurial.

Mr. Booker also owned a barber shop, which was the social gathering place where the men gathered for community news and gossip.

Mr. Booker was tall and had a loud laugh that could be heard throughout the neighborhood. His famous trademark was his cigar that hung from his lips as he cut the hair of his customers on Saturday mornings.

His wife, Miss Savanna, short, muscular and tough, was known for no nonsense. One Saturday morning, a man came into the store staggering drunkenly with slurred speech and cursing up a storm. "Gotdammit, woman, git yo' big ass behind that counter and gimme a pack of cigarettes," he said.

Miss Savanna approached the man, grabbed him by the collar and shouted, "Look here, buddy, I don't 'low no cussin' in my sto', 'specially in front of little chilluns." The man recognized the seriousness in Miss Savanna's eyes: "Yessum, Miss Savanna. You know I didn't mean no harm," he said as he quickly backed out the door.

Saturday was a day of play, relaxation, and movies. If your parents felt that you had done your chores properly, they would reward you with a small allowance of ten or fifteen cents to go uptown to Springhill to the movies. The theater, located on the main street, featured Western cowboy movies and continuing adventure series of famous heroes who led you back each week to see the outcomes.

Our movie heroes were white movie stars: Roy Rogers, Gene Autry, John Wayne, Wild Bill Hickok, the Phantom, Captain Marvel and Superman. Black characters such as Stepin Fetchit were always portrayed as negative stereotypes, acting as domestics, clowns, buffoons, with mannerisms of laziness, slang speech and child-like antics.

Saturday was pay day and Saturday night was a special night in small-town rural, Black America. Whiskey, wine and women attracted the pleasure-seeking crowd from the town and backwood areas. During this period, every able-bodied person was employed. There was no unemployment or welfare. The night was a time of releasing the tension of five and a half days of hard labor from the scorching hot sun in the cotton fields, saw mills, paper factory and back wood timbering. It was getting away from the mean-spirited overseers and "po' white folks." Every small, rural southern community had its saloons, gambling joints, greasy spoon cafes, prostitute houses and barbecue joints where a man named "Barbecue Slim" had the best barbecue in town. They drank, gambled, danced, talked loud, threw bottles and settled long-standing feuds, generally resulting from unpaid gambling debts and lovers' quarrels.

Our house was on the edge of this bustling area. The jukeboxes sounded through the night, with sounds of famous blues singers who had their early start in these establishments. The recordings of such blues singers as Little Jimmy Reed, John Lee Hooker, Bessie Smith, Louis Jordan and Muddy Waters dominated the airwaves of the juke joints. Jordan's popular song was "Let the Good Times Roll."

After such nights of revelry, it was not unusual to learn the next morning of an occasional knifing. Crime was contained in the small section of town. It was generally ignored by the local sheriff, since it was "jest niggers killing niggers." Muh was afraid on Saturday nights. She longed for the small, rural community where she was reared.

Sunday morning was much more to Muh's liking, but because ministers pastored at more than one church in the parish, services normally were held only twice per month. During the off-Sundays, my brother and I would join the other boys of the community and attend the baseball games of the Cullen Tigers, a local black baseball team owned and operated by Booker Tatum. Mr. Booker was the brother of the famous "Goose Tatum," a star with the Harlem Globetrotters and the Cincinnati Clowns baseball team. Black men could not play on the nationally organized white baseball, basketball or football teams during this period. Black athletes, such as Joe Louis, the world heavyweight boxing champion and Sugar Ray Robinson, the welterweight boxing champion, were our idols. They had broken the racial shackles with their muscles and fists. They wore the crown of glory, and earned it by fighting from poverty to fame.

The Cullen Tigers was part of an organized Negro Baseball League, which included teams from other cities such as Minden, Shreveport and Bastrop in Louisiana; and Camden and Eldorado, Arkansas. These teams produced exciting athletic events, attracting black as well as white fans. Black athletes provided an extra dimension to baseball through their clowning plays and fancy tricks.

As World War II progressed, there was an increasing demand for manpower. As a result, many of the young talented players were drafted into the segregated armed forces to fight for their country.

The beginning of 1943 was a down period for the family. Muh became seriously ill. Even during her illness, she would rise early and push herself to do a day's work. Her health was slowly failing. Healthcare for black folks during this period was nonexistent. Mama Caroline came to her rescue. She tried to care for her with the "ole folks'" medical remedies, which further aggravated her illness.

On March 4, 1943, Dad came to school to take my brother and me to live with Mama Caroline during Muh's illness. The acuteness of her illness led to her hospitalization at the Charity Hospital in Shreveport where she quietly passed on the early morning of March 6, 1943. The cause of her death was probably a combination of untreated diabetes and high blood pressure. During the night of Muh's death, I dreamt that our house had burned to the ground. Smoke and ashes flashed before my eyes. When I awoke, I shared the dream with my brother.

A daze came over me as we boarded the Greyhound bus to return home. Finding no seats in the back of the bus where blacks were legally required to sit, I took a seat near the middle of the bus in the section reserved for whites. Looking through his mirror, the bus driver, a white man in his forties, spotted me. He got up and headed down the aisle with a mean look on his face. He demanded in a loud voice that I remove myself from the seat and stand in the aisle, since all the seats reserved for blacks were filled. Though only 8 years old, I refused to move. In his anger, he shouted out at me, "Nigger boy, git yo' black ass out of that seat." I became very upset and refused again to give up my seat. Upon hearing the bus driver's demand for a second time, an old black couple rushed to the middle of the bus and quickly grabbed me by the arm and escorted me to sit between them on the back seat of the bus. They knew that I could have been killed for defying the orders of a white man. It was the same fear that I saw in my father's eyes when he restrained me from throwing rocks at the white sheriff's car as he passed the house.

It was a cold morning when we got off the bus and started the long walk home. As we approached our house, we saw a crowd of people, some of them searching through the ashes of our home. A next door tenant left a cigarette burning on a table near her bed, causing our home to be destroyed. My dream had become reality.

Dad came out to meet us with a hug and a saddened face, telling us the bad news that Muh had passed away during the early morning hour at the same time that our house had burned into ashes. The news of Muh's passing and the loss of our home were a double-edged sword. The lightning and thunder had struck again. Muh died at the young age of 28. She worked hard all of her young life. At eight years old, I felt a sense of loss and despair that God had betrayed me. It was so painful that I could not cry.

Muh was short, stocky, strongly built, with a dark complexion, deep dimples and a smile always on her face. She was soft spoken, a woman of few words. Like many rural black women of her time, she viewed herself working alongside her husband as a co-provider of the family, a tradition passed down from slavery and Reconstruction.

Muh's funeral was held at the Growing Valley Missionary Baptist Church, where she had been baptized and married by the Rev. Jessie Dixon. Now he was presiding over her funeral. Her casket was placed on a mule-driven wagon team and drawn to her final resting place in the old McDonald Cemetery near the McDonald Plantation. My brother and I were left in the care of Dad and Big Mama. Mama Caroline requested Dad to allow us to live with her. Dad refused the offer and vowed to raise his boys.

However, Big Mama was aging and could no longer fully care for her two grandsons. Dad was introduced to a nice lady by Aunt Ruthann, my mother's sister, and by family friend, Emma Sims. Our new mother was Willie Mae Wilson, a divorcee without children. Dad had not known her before Muh's death. He entered into his second marriage on May 25, 1943. She was an attractive 36-year-old lady who quickly took my brother and me into her loving care. The family regrouped and bonded.

Shortly after their marriage, Mama and Dad moved to Many, Louisiana, in search of work in the pulp wood cutting industry. My brother and I were again left in the care of Big Mama, who was always there for us. Unable to find satisfactory work in Louisiana, Dad, along with other friends, left to find employment in the naval shipyard at Patuxent, Maryland, near the city of Baltimore. This was short lived. The United States' Selective Service Board summoned him for examination for induction into the armed forces. The family was happy when he did not pass his physical examination due to a heart murmur. Dad left Louisiana for a second time and headed west to work in the Kaiser Shipyard at Richmond, California, in the San Francisco Bay area.

Shortly after his departure, Big Mama became seriously ill in March 1944. A fatal shooting occurred next door to our residence. Our neighbor Emmet Bridley was killed by a man named Cleo Cave in a lover's quarrel. Cave was a baseball player with the Cullen Tigers. This greatly upset Big Mama. She already had experienced a series of painful events: the death of her daughter-in-law a year earlier and the departure of her son. This was too much for her to bear in her old age.

Our new mother had gone to care for her aging mother, Sarah Chatman Cook/Wilson, who was suffering from symptoms that we know today as Alzheimer's disease. During Mama's absence, Big Mama was placed in the care of her brother, Uncle Bill Hamilton and his wife Elonia who lived in Couchwood, Louisiana. On April 4, 1944, Big Mama passed away. She died at age 67 on her birthday.

Big Mama's passing was a blow to me. She had been my nurturer, teacher and mentor during my short lifetime. She was the stabilizing force for my brother and me. We loved her dearly. She was the most significant person in our early childhood.

She shared her life story of growing up during the period of Reconstruction. "There were towns in Louisiana where blacks were not allowed after sunset. Signs were posted reading: 'Niggers, read and run, and if you can't read, you better run like hell!'" she told us. There were stories of hangings and lynching of black men. These were the storms of her lifetime.

Dad returned from California to lay Big Mama to rest. She had adopted and cared for him as an infant and reared him to manhood. Her funeral also took place at the Growing Valley Missionary Baptist Church, where she was eulogized by Rev. Dixon. Her remains were laid to rest in the McDonald Cemetery, the cemetery of the slave ancestors.

Dad returned to Richmond, California, and left us in the care of our new mother. As we prepared to join Dad in Richmond, my

mind wandered to happier times in the small twin towns of Cullen/
Springhill before Muh passed.

My Parents

Dad (1909-1991) & Muh   (1915-1943)

Dad and second Mother Willie Mae
Wilson/Phillips (1907-1987)

Big Mama Lula Hamilton/Phillips, Me and Childhood
friends at Cullen/Springhill, LA 1942

Left: Me in 1942

Right: My brother
Andrew 1939

Dad and his Father, Grandfather Ellis
Harris (1896-1968) at Minneapolis

Aunt Ruthann Warren/Thomas,
First mother's sister (1918-1990)

Dad and favorite Uncle S.J. Waller, Sr. (1900-2004)

Parents and Relatives

From left to right: Dad's brother and sister;

Dad (1909-1991), Aunt Mary Lee/Scott (1901-
1993), Uncle Eugene Lee (1898-1984)

Dad's sister, Aunt Rosie Lee/
Jenkins/Johnson (1906-1994)

CHAPTER SIX

The Great Western Migration

Like the exodus of the Hebrews out of Egypt, the period of World War II witnessed the beginning of the second large migration of blacks from the rural South to western, northern and eastern seaboard states to work in war-related industries.

* * *

In April 1944, Dad sent for us to join him in Richmond, California. Mama, my brother, nicknamed Webb, and I packed the family's meager belongings and prepared to take the long journey to the West coast. The departure was mixed with sadness and joy. Sadness came from bidding farewell to relatives and childhood friends. Joy came from the thought of the family being together again.

The evening of departure attracted a large gathering of friends and relatives at the small train depot. I had grown to cherish the green pastures, tall yellow pines, oaks, hickory nut trees, and wild cherries and grapes in the bayous and wooded areas. Waving hands, teary eyes and warm embraces showered us as the smokestack iron horse slowly pulled away from the station. The rail, which had brought some of my slave ancestors to the Deep South, now moved the family westward.

Traveling west was a long and tedious journey during the war years. The passenger trains and Greyhound buses were the major sources of mass transportation. The Southern Pacific Rail route took us through the cities of Texarkana, Arkansas; Houston and El Paso, Texas; Los Angeles, and north to the bay area city of Richmond. This journey of three days and three nights seemed endless to a child nine years of age.

The train was packed with soldiers, sailors, Marines and non-military families. Mama instructed Webb and me to stay near her and refrain from talking to strangers.

Blacks and whites rode in separate train cars until we reached El Paso, a transfer point, where Jim Crow segregation ended. We traveled across the rolling plains that stretched for hundreds of miles across the state of Texas with its large ranches of cattle, horses and other livestock roaming the open plains.

During the war years, traveling was regulated in favor of military personnel. When a maximum number of civilian travelers passed through certain exits, gates were closed, restricting the further flow of traffic. Civilian passengers had to be especially alert to exit the gates quickly to board the next train. My brother was awed by the large crowd of people who crammed through the gates before they closed. When Mama and I looked around, we discovered that my brother had not made it in time. We returned and remained until the next morning for another train heading west. That time, my brother was the first one out of the gate. He stood with a smile on his face waiting for us to join him.

As the train pulled from the station, I saw what appeared to be elevated slopes in the distance. These were mountains, which I had never seen before. They rose majestically above the Great Plains, commanding a presence over the rugged landscape. It appeared that we would never reach the foot of the great Southern Rockies as we entered New Mexico.

This was truly God's country. His handiwork appeared in the deep valleys, carved out by running streams and rivers of a million years in the making. The scenery was breathtaking as the train engine pulled the cars in the winding rail path of the sloping mountains.

The rocks along the mountainsides were rugged and folded. At times, it was frightening looking down the deep valley gorges, partially darkened by the shadows of the mountain slopes bathed by a beautiful evening sunset. A rainbow arched gracefully from sunlight passing through a rain shower. The spectacular view sent chills of awe through my body in realization of the supreme God of creation.

The approaching night brought a curtain of darkness and the sound of the train engine echoed from the mountainside. The rhythmical sound of the train wheels rolling against the rails was the last sound that I heard as sleep fell over my eyes.

We finally arrived at Richmond. Dad came to meet and warmly embrace us. We unloaded our belongings and headed to our new home. Things were different. We were surrounded by a mountain range on the east and the bay and ocean on the west. The houses were different. They were rental project housing, framed, two-story apartment complexes, all looking the same. Each housing complex was divided into four sectional apartment units, two downstairs and two upstairs. Each apartment unit contained three small bedrooms, a single bath, kitchen and living room/dining area combined. We were not accustomed to using indoor toilets.

Housing was scarce and families had to share space until more housing became available. Three families shared the apartment unit; Cousin Curtis Coulter and his wife; Mr. Bubba and Nancy Alexander; and our family. Dad had made arrangements to live with his cousin and wife prior to moving the family. Each family in the unit took turns preparing meals, washing and ironing.

Because children of the housing project had no organized play area, the streets and sidewalks became the playgrounds. We organized ourselves into teams. Our favorite games were stick ball and hide-and-seek. A broomstick was used for a bat, and a small Pet Milk can for a ball. The light poles were used for bases. Play time would extend into the night until our parents called us indoors. Dad had a standing rule that my brother and I had to be inside at the setting of the sun.

There were many children in the neighborhood. I developed a crush on the girl next door. She was rough as any boy in the neighborhood. She could fight you toe-to-toe. Mama could tell the number of fights I engaged in by the number of torn shirts she had to patch each week.

During the evenings and the weekends, the adults would sit around and talk, play dominoes or bid whist while the children played until bedtime. My brother and I slept on a small cot in the kitchen/dining area. Our apartment was on Earlerson Street, near the railroad tracks, which separated the black and white sections of town.

Although the housing was segregated, all children attended the same neighborhood school. My brother and I enrolled at Stege Elementary School during the fall of 1944. The school was racially diverse, including blacks, whites, Asians, Hispanics and Native Americans. Japanese children were visibly absent because they had been moved inland by the U.S. government and placed in camps, mainly in Montana and Utah. The government imposed the war policy, alleging a fear of sabotage by Japanese Americans, the majority of whom were natural born Americans of Japanese descent. This was not the case with German or Italian Americans whose mother countries were also at war against us.

Many of the whites in the area were migrants from southern and mid-western states. They migrated during the dust droughts from the states of Oklahoma, Arkansas, Missouri and Kansas.

Our teachers were mainly white females. There were no teachers of color during this period. The curriculum centered on the heroes and heroines of the dominant culture. In this new, integrated situation, the teachers provided more attention to white students. I do not remember ever being called upon to perform any academic exercise. The only activity for which I was recognized was my running ability during recess.

The schools were vastly overcrowded to the extent that children attended school in double shifts; one half during a morning shift and the other half during the afternoon shift. Children were required to perform air raid drills and other emergency exercises in preparation of an enemy attack.

My brother and I developed a shoeshine business. We would rise early Saturday morning and walk downtown with our shoeshine boxes to solicit sales up and down McDonald Avenue, the main street of the town. Shoppers filled the streets. Our best customers were military personnel who were required to maintain their shoes in excellent shining order. They were good tippers, especially those who were intoxicated. They would often give you a dollar bill and forget their change. The cost of a shoeshine was ten cents, fifteen cents if you applied a special dressing to the shoe soles.

By noon, we had earned enough money to attend a movie. Movie theaters would not allow you to take your shoeshine box inside. One Saturday, I was so eager to attend a movie that I took a chance and hid my box in a street garbage container. When I returned, all of my supplies had been removed from my box. My parents teased me all week until I earned enough money to replenish my supplies.

To earn additional income, I delivered groceries for shoppers at neighborhood stores after school. I constructed a cart from fruit crates and abandoned tricycle wheels. This was a creative invention for hauling groceries to the homes of people in the neighborhood. I earned about two dollars a week between my two work activities. We used our money to go to the movies and buy candy. Despite all of our entrepreneurial activities, we still had leisure time, especially during the summer months, to get into mischief.

During the summer of 1945, the family moved into its own apartment in the Pullman Housing Projects along Jefferson Avenue. Dad and Mama were both working during the midnight shift. A cousin next door attended to Webb and me during the night. The absence of grandparents or older persons to care for us created some problems. There were other children in the neighborhood who faced the same circumstances.

A group of friends and I organized a small neighborhood gang. We built ourselves a gang hideout made from cardboard boxes in an underdeveloped open field area near the shores of the bay. We were able to slip in and out of the area unnoticed due to the high overgrowth of seaweed. One day we planned and organized a raid on a nearby grocery store located on a highway near the open field. First, a scouting party would case the store, particularly to determine the level of activity during certain hours of the day. We determined the best time to make our hit. A couple of boys were sent to engage the store owner while others would slip into the rear of the store and stock our bags full of candies, cakes and soft drinks. This activity ceased when the store owner caught us in the act and threatened to call the police and our parents!

We were terrified. We pleaded with the owner to allow us to unload a train boxcar loaded with watermelons to pay for our mischief. He accepted our offer, and that ended our short criminal career. I experienced a feeling of guilt for my mischief. Mother and Dad had taught me never to take anyone's property.

Uncle Larry, Mother's nephew, had become a minister. He persuaded Mother and Dad to allow my brother and me to attend revival meetings that were held in his home. He persuaded us, through his preaching, to confess our sins and become saved and delivered from "hell fire and brimstone." This frightened me into accepting the call to join church at the age of 10. Mama told Uncle Larry that I was too young to understand what I was doing. This religious confession was postponed until the age of 12.

Racial confrontations between blacks and whites were low key during the war years although racial incidents often flared up at our integrated schools.

One hot day in July 1945, a rumor circulated within the black housing project that a black soldier had been shot near the white housing project. A crowd of black youth from the community gathered at the base of the rock quarry that separated the two communities, resulting in rock throwing between white and black youths. Further tension was created by a white female who appeared at the top of the quarry with a rifle and began firing bullets into the air. The police were quickly summoned to quell the disturbance. Shortly afterward, a branch of the NAACP was formed to investigate racial confrontations.

After this incident, the leadership of the school community initiated a patriotic school festival that brought together the school children to sing and group dance with the words, "Jump, jump, jump, jump, Jim Crow. Jump, jump and away we go." These activities took place when the war in Europe was coming to an end.

Families were required to make many sacrifices during the war years. Goods that were essential to the maintenance of the war effort were rationed. A freeze was placed on the sale of many food products. Families were issued ration stamp books to buy such foods as butter, meats, sugar, rubber and metals. To keep a supply of these goods,

Mama would awaken my brother and me early on Saturday mornings to stand in long lines to purchase enough food for the family.

The housing shortage caused the family to share its space with other families moving from the South to work and earn enough money to send for other family members back home. Our apartment complex became the social gathering place for many families coming west.

While playing in the backyard in May 1945, the sound of sirens, bells, car and bus horns sent a blast through the air. People ran into the streets, displaying great emotions, waving flags in celebration that the Germans, under the Nazi leader Adolph Hitler, had surrendered.

Newspaper pictures showed the great devastation of war - human bodies piled in heaps near Nazi concentration camps where millions of European Jews and others were killed by Hitler and his Nazi henchmen in the Holocaust. The tragedy illustrated the evils of war and the inhumanity of the human species.

CHAPTER SEVEN

The Aftermath Of War:
Northern Migration

The end of the war signaled an end to the great demand for the unskilled and semiskilled labor in the war-related industries, resulting in a great downsizing of the labor force and massive layoffs of millions of workers. As usual, the last hired were the first fired. Some black families moved back South while others moved into the farming valley communities of Fresno, Bakersfield and Stockton for the open spaces they had been accustomed to in the old South.

* * *

Dad was among those who found themselves unemployed.

During the summer of 1946, Dad decided to send Webb and me back home in the care of our mother, who already had returned to Louisiana to care for her aging mother. A relative accompanied us on the long journey. We prepared the traveling meal, consisting of fried chicken and pound cake, carefully packed in a shoe box. Conditions had not changed for blacks. Even though blacks had fought bravely and lost their lives to "save the world for democracy," they still could not eat in white-owned restaurants. It was ironic to see that our enemies had greater access to opportunities than we had in our homeland.

Dad later returned after being unsuccessful in finding employment in the Richmond/Oakland Bay area. The family eventually returned to the Cullen/Springhill community. Dad and Mother used their savings to purchase land and housing.

Mama's aging mother, Grandma Sarah Chatman Cook/Wilson, took residence with us. She was now 83, having been born on September 10, 1863. She had owned 80 acres of farm land in the Longview farming community near the town of Benton, Louisiana. The family had borrowed funds from the Freedman's Bank during Reconstruction to assist in the purchase. In 1946, the parish government, under the guise of eminent domain, condemned the family farm land for flood runoff control. It was discovered later that the land was converted to a game and hunting reserve. The family had no recourse with the courts to reclaim the land.

It was difficult for black men to find steady employment after the war. Dad hired himself out as a pulp woodcutter in the timbering industry. He also used his skill as a bricklayer to assist a local black merchant to build a furniture store and lumberyard.

We re-enrolled in the Cullen Colored Elementary School. The black men of the community built a new three-room school to replace the old Baptist church school. The new school was built behind the newly constructed First Missionary Baptist Church.

My brother and I became active in the youth church after confessing Christ and being baptized in 1946 by the pastor, the Rev. A.W. Grant. In addition to our parents, our early mentors included our public and Sunday School teachers and the deacons of the church. They were: Ella Fair Webb, Willie Mae Williams, elementary school teachers; and deacons Leroy Bolden and Earl Davidson.

Unable to find steady employment in Cullen, Dad returned to California to work with his uncle, S.J. Waller, who had become a building contractor in Fresno. Dad later purchased land in Fresno with intentions of moving his family back west.

Time appeared to move slowly for a boy of eleven. Circumstances were difficult for the family. Mama was unable to work since she had to care for her aging mother. Grandma had become unruly. Her Alzheimer's condition had worsened. Her mind drifted back to the days of slavery and Reconstruction. She talked about working on the massa's land as a child.

To earn enough money until Dad was able to send money home, Mama took in washing and ironing from white families. During the summer months, Webb hired himself out, cutting lawns for the township sheriff until one day he was framed for allegedly stealing the sheriff's lawn mower. Mama became greatly upset when the sheriff came to our home in search of the mower. He approached mama on the front porch one evening.

"Willie Mae," he said, "I'm jest coming by to see if yo' boy might have brought my lawn mower heah."

"No sir, Mr. Nixon, you ain't gwine find no mower heah. We don't even have no grass heah to mow," she said.

The white family mama washed for later cleared my brother's name. Black males had little or no credibility when their claim of veracity conflicted with that of a white man, especially, the township sheriff. Mama cautioned my brother never to cut grass for the sheriff again.

Just prior to 1947, the automotive industry up North was beginning to boom. The demand for labor in the industry was increasing as the big motor giants: General Motors, Ford and Chrysler increased production.

Mama received word from her cousin in Michigan that work was becoming plentiful in the factories and foundries. Dad returned home, sold his property holdings of two houses and a vacant lot and headed for Muskegon Heights, a booming industrial city located along Lake Michigan in western Michigan. The twin cities of Muskegon and Muskegon Heights housed a manufacturing center for the production of automotive, aircraft and refrigeration parts and services. Dad readily found employment in a local foundry and sent for the family to join him in the spring of 1947.

Since Mama was the caretaker for her mother, we had to arrange to take her with us. Grandma Sarah Chatman Cook/Wilson had developed a strong bond with me. I had been assigned to assist Mama in caring for her, taking her food, cleaning her room, emptying her slop jar and getting her out of bed to sit during the day.

When we got ready to leave for Michigan, we had to trick her into leaving. She did not want to leave. We informed her that she was being taken back to her farm.

During the day of our departure, Mama became very nervous with fear that Grandma would run away. When we boarded the train, she sat Grandma near me. Mama said, "Little Joe, hold tightly to yo' Grandma's hand when we change trains in St. Louis, Missouri."

St. Louis was the point where Jim Crow segregation ended heading north. When we reached St. Louis, there were many people in the train station hurrying to change trains. Moving among the large crowd of people, Grandma became confused and resistant. She commented that someone in the crowd was beckoning her to follow in another direction. At that moment, she began to walk away from us. I gently grabbed her hand and encouraged her to follow us. She obeyed and we were off to the next train heading north to Chicago.

After two days and two nights of travel, we reached our destination. We were glad to see Dad, who met us at the station with Mama's cousin, who was driving a new car.

Housing was scarce. Dad had rented a small room in a single residence that housed several families and single men. Like us, they had moved to the area to work in the foundries and factories. Webb and I shared a sleeping cot in the hallway.

We had to rise early each morning to allow people who worked at night to take their turn sleeping during the day. Each family took turns preparing their meals and doing their laundry. Some of the younger couples spent a great amount of time arguing, fussing and invading the privacy of other families over petty matters.

After living in these overcrowded arrangements with uncooperative landlords, high rents and leaking roofs, Dad used his meager savings to purchase a small plot of land to build a home near the outskirts of the city. To be near the property, Dad rented a garage from a friend and his wife. He converted the garage to make living arrangements consisting of a kitchen area and a combined sleeping and socialization area. An old kerosene stove was used for cooking and heating during the cold winter of 1948.

That year Harry S. Truman came from behind, defeated John Dewey and was elected President. During the campaign, the

Democratic Party and the United Auto Workers brought heavyweight boxing champion Joe Louis to town to rally the black vote. This election raised the level of national consciousness and acknowledged the growing black vote in urban areas.

The Korean conflict was looming on the horizon as the economy was beginning to transition into a post-war era of cold war with Russia and an emerging Red China. The international conflict again expanded employment opportunities for the many unskilled and semiskilled veterans returning from World War II.

In addition to working full time in the foundry, Dad supplemented his income with part-time employment at a local cement plant. He used his extra income to purchase materials for the house he wanted to build. Dad bought the materials in small installments. Assisting him after school and during the weekend, my brother and I gained knowledge of the construction trades.

Just prior to the Christmas holidays in 1948, we had finished enough of the construction to move into our new home. It was the best Christmas present that the family received. This experience taught us Dad's philosophy: "Save your money, get a good education, practice independence and never be without land or a home of your own."

My brother and I enrolled at Muskegon Heights Central Junior High School. There were no more second hand books or equipment handed down from white schools. Black and white children shared the same programs and facilities on an equal basis.

The school was a modern, red brick building located along the main street of town. It contained well-equipped classrooms, vocational and science laboratories, a cafeteria, gymnasium and a large play area, including a track, tennis courts, football and softball fields. Students came from middle- and working-class family backgrounds. Parents earned their incomes in the foundries, small manufacturing plants, tool shops, and retail stores of the area. Black students were primarily the first generation of students from the South, mostly from Louisiana, Arkansas, Mississippi and Texas. The majority of the white students were children of parents who had come from western Europe - England, Ireland, Germany, Scotland and the Netherlands. There also was a sizable number of students whose families were from Poland, Hungary, Italy, Greece, Czechoslovakia and Yugoslavia. The community was reflective of small-town, middle America during the 1940s and `50s. All of our teachers were white. If any had any racial animosities, they were not glaring.

The climate and tone of the high school were set by an outstanding principal of Dutch descent. We called him "Father C.F. Bolt." Upon reaching high school in 1951, he took a special interest in my future. During the summer months, I did his lawn maintenance. He encouraged me to study hard, get good grades and be a role model for other black students.

Even though the school was physically integrated, white and black students kept their social distance. Interracial fraternization outside and within the school environment was not an acceptable practice. Friendship patterns generally developed around the school athletic program. Black students were visibly absent from the school drama program but were highly encouraged to participate in the athletic and music programs, which included football, basketball, baseball, track, tennis, band and vocal music. The school had an outstanding athletic program for males but not for females.

Ninth grade was a turning point in my life. I had become a serious student. I was elected vice president of the student council. There was a high level of expectation from my teachers and parents to succeed. This kept me motivated to walk the right path. I became active in the high school athletic program, which was a powerhouse in the Southwestern Michigan conference. The conference included competitive high schools in Muskegon, Grand Rapids, Holland, Benton Harbor, Grand Haven and Kalamazoo.

High school sports were big events that drew the entire town on Friday nights. During my junior and senior years, I became an outstanding running back. I also lettered in basketball and baseball.

During the summer months, I participated in the American Legion Baseball League. It was often a lonely feeling being the only black player. Catcalls would sometimes be directed by members of the opposing team and the crowd: "Get that nigger off the field. He don't belong here!" I ignored these remarks and continued to hit home runs that beat our opponents. Additionally, my white teammates would rally behind me. My spiritual values, deep faith in God and myself provided a shield for me to rise above acts of disrespect.

The church continued to play a significant role in my development. Dad served as a role model. He became a deacon at the Friendship Missionary Baptist Church, a rural, southern church planted north. Webb and I were ordained as junior deacons and became young leaders within the church. By the age of fifteen, I became a biblical scholar and a Sunday school teacher of both young people and adults. I read and had a command of Biblical history and theology. This led me to an interest in education and teaching.

I found myself becoming a religious zealot to the extent that my friends referred to me as "preacher". During football trips out of town, I would keep the boys in line from using excessive profanity and rowdiness. The spiritual aspects of my life influenced my personal relationships. My choice of friends was those who studied and took an interest in their personal development.

But an extreme case of acne caused me to become shy and withdrawn in my social relationships. I spent a great deal of time with my mother. She viewed me as "her baby" and showered me with her love and care. We spent many hours together in the kitchen. She taught me all the chores of housekeeping. I assisted her in washing, cooking and laundry activities.

Mama was not too keen on my football activities. She was afraid that I would get hurt. Dad had become a custodian at the high school during my senior year, which gave him an opportunity to see me play at each of the home games. This calmed Mama's fears.

When girls began to enter my life, my parents became protective of the types of girls with whom I associated. Girls they perceived as being "too fast" or not from a reputable family were a no-no in their eyes. I fell in love with the preacher's daughter and later found that she was one of the swiftest girls in town when not in her parents' sight.

The Korean conflict was winding down and some of my high school friends were dropping out to join the military. Work was in abundance. Webb and I acquired employment in a local metal plating factory owned by Don Wershem, a white merchant and an alumnus of the high school. He allowed us to work after school and during the summer months.

It was not all work, there was some play. The lakes and white beaches became favorite hangouts during the hot summer months. The clean fresh waters provided an opportunity to swim and have fun. After learning to swim and develop confidence in the deeper parts of the lake, I decided to swim to a diving platform located a distance from the lake's shore. I was doing great until I tried to pull myself onto the platform. It was extremely slippery and I lost my grip and found myself underneath the platform. I remained calm and did not panic. After coming up for a third time, I saw hands of white swimmers reaching for me and pulling me up on the platform. I gained my composure and confidence and swam back to shore. That was a close call.

As summer ended, we knew it was time to gear up for the long hours of practice and drilling to get in shape for the football season. The year was 1952, my senior year. The season started with high expectations of a championship year. The team was in high spirits. Our first game was with Grand Rapids Catholic Central, a team with a great reputation as state champions. It was the team to beat. We were the underdogs, having to play on their field.

That Friday night game attracted more than 2,000 fans. On the first play of the game, I took the handoff from the quarterback Kenneth Plichta on a right-half dive. After receiving a block from the right tackle Kenneth Tuttle and right guard, Joe Laban, I scampered to the sidelines as the fans stood on their feet and watched me carry the ball to the 10-yard line. My legs cramped, causing me to be hit from behind before reaching the end zone. On the next play, fullback Arnold Ochs took the ball over for a touchdown. It was a big victory that resulted in serious injuries to two of our top players: fullback Arnold Ochs and left end Louis McMurray. Without them, the team was unable to sustain a consistent series of victories.

After football season, I had a serious parting of the ways with the head football coach, who also coached basketball. I informed him that I would be unable to play my final season on the basketball team because I wanted to obtain an after-school job to help support the family, which had fallen on hard times with the building of the family home. The coach became very upset with me. One day after school, he approached me in the locker room and started an argument. He then grabbed me by the collar and demanded that I clean out my locker and never return to his gym again. He further announced that I would not receive recommendations for scholarships to play college football. I informed him that my college future did not depend upon receiving an athletic scholarship because I had already received two college academic scholarships.

Achieving the 15th position in the class ranking provided me an opportunity to receive scholarships from the Muskegon Rotary Club and the Tri-Cities Women's Club. I followed the advice of my father to never place all your eggs in one basket, but spread your talents to other pursuits. It was the way that Big Mama and my early teachers had taught me: "Stay two steps ahead of the game and do not allow others to control your vision." My brother, who had graduated two years previous, decided on other alternatives for himself.

A serious family breach had developed between my brother and our parents. Dad and Mama had strict rules regarding our going and coming, especially at night. The rule was that we had to be home by a certain hour at night. My brother had now become fully employed. In addition to this, he had enrolled at the local junior college. Since a child, he had a strong sense of independence and was a free spirit. He refused to adjust to my parents' rules. Dad said, "There's only one head of the household and that is me. If you cannot abide by my rules, you pick up and leave." My brother packed up his clothing and found himself another residence.

I was deeply saddened by his departure. We had been together since infancy. After he left, we kept in touch with each other, and I attempted to reconcile the differences for him to return. The schism was too deep to repair. During my senior year, Webb joined the Air Force and I did not see him again until 1960 when we both had begun our own families.

Upon graduation, I made a choice to attend the Muskegon Junior College to commence a career in either medicine or education. I had been strongly advised by my high school economics teacher to study to become a teacher and return to teach in my hometown. My choice of colleges was limited by the family's financial resources and those that I had acquired from my scholarships and savings. The University of Minnesota at Minneapolis became an option when Dad's natural father made contact and visited us during the summer of 1953. Dad had never known his natural father since he had left Louisiana just after his birth.

Like many black men, Ellis Harris left Louisiana during the first black migration out of the South following World War I. He took a job as a Pullman porter and eventually settled in Minneapolis. He married and later served as an assistant minister at a Baptist church in St. Paul. He also served at a church in North Dakota. In addition to his ministry, he worked as a porter at Sheik's Department Store in downtown Minneapolis.

My grandfather's visit established the beginning of a bond between the two families. During the summer of 1954, I visited with Grandpa Ellis and his wife Lucy. They lived comfortably in a lovely home in Minneapolis in a quiet, tree-lined neighborhood. He died in the late 1960s.

Most black high school graduates during the 1950s had limited options: working in unskilled jobs in the local factories or foundries, volunteering for the military, going to college, or becoming involved in the numbers racket, trying to become rich quickly. I attended the local junior college so that I could work and save enough to attend a four-year college.

The college classes were small. All the professors were white. They were outstanding except for my biology teacher, who was considered an odd ball. No matter how hard I worked in his class, I could never earn a grade higher than a "C". In fact, my final grade was a "D," the only one I ever obtained in either high school or college. I resolved to move this mental shackle from my psychic by pursuing a career in the biological sciences.

One of the most outstanding and popular professors at the college befriended me and eventually became my mentor. Dr. John McKinley, a professor of history and political science, encouraged me to select Eastern Michigan University at Ypsilanti, an outstanding teachers' college. He arranged for me to obtain a Michigan State Board of Education scholarship to pursue a four-year degree in secondary education. Other exciting things began to unfold for me.

During the winter of 1954, I met a young lady named Vira L. Goosby through my friend Leroy Mitchell, who was engaged to marry one of Vira's sisters, Elizabeth Paschal. The occasion was a going away party for Leroy, who was entering the military. I had prayed to God to meet a young lady with whom I could share a mutual interest. We had lived in the same small town, but had never met. She was still in high school during my first year in college. My eyes were attracted to her during the party. We were both a little shy; however, my desire to know her better persuaded me to ask her for a dance. After our first dance, I danced with her several times.

After the party, I asked the usual question: "May I have your phone number to call you sometimes?" She smiled, rolled her large beautiful eyes and answered in a soft tone, "I guess so." In addition to her beautiful dark brown eyes, she possessed coffee-creamed colored skin, a round shaped face with long black curly hair. I spent the night planning to meet her again. The next day, I called and we agreed to a theater date. We became attracted to each other and our romance began.

Vira and I came from similar rural backgrounds. Her family had migrated to Michigan in 1946 from the small town of Magnolia, Arkansas, located approximately thirty miles north of Cullen/ Springhill. Her father and mother, Pierce Goosby and Willie Mae McGraw/Goosby, shared twenty children, some from their previous marriages. Her father had been a farmer before moving to Muskegon Heights. He, like other black men, had migrated to the area to work in the local foundry. Her grandfather, Calvin Goosby, owned a farm near the town of Magnolia. He was a rugged individualist who did not take any "shit from racist white men." This got him in trouble with certain white men of the small rural community. As a result of this difficulty, he was lynched by a mob of white men in the early 1900s. The family was later forced to give up its land and enter the sharecropping system.

During the summer of 1954, I obtained a job in the local foundry to earn money for my college education. Work in a foundry was mainly unskilled, back breaking, repetitive and labor intensive. I was assigned to work inside the foundry while my white college peers worked outside or in office-related work. I worked with the overhead crane operator, hooking up buckets of hot, molten iron and other materials that were transported throughout the foundry.

The best description of a foundry is a "hell dungeon" on Earth. It was a place where men worked near hot furnaces; where pig iron was dumped into heated furnaces and melted down into molten iron and later poured into large bricked-lined cast iron buckets; where men worked on shake-out machines, removing the finished products from the patterns, and on grinding machines, grinding down the rough surfaces of the motor blocks. It was a place filled with dirt, smoke, heat and deafening noise; it was a place of fork lift trucks, lifting and loading motor products into trucks and freight cars, moving the finished products to assembly plants in Detroit, Flint and other destinations of automotive manufacturing; it was a place where men assembled to earn a hard living in unbearable conditions. Foremost, I viewed it as a corporate plantation system without leg irons and chains.

The work force and management hierarchy reflected the racial and socio-economic profile of the manufacturing system of corporate America of the fifties and sixties. Upper-, middle- and first-line managers were all white males. The technicians and skilled craftsmen were sprinkled with a few blacks, but for the most part, they were mainly white males. The unskilled and semiskilled workforce was poor whites, immigrants and blacks. Office workers consisted of white males and females.

To relax from the routine repetition of the work, the workmen developed games of "horse play," which consisted of dashing each other with buckets of water, stuffing tools or their hands into the rear end of fellow workers. A most prevalent practice was the heavy use of profanity, joking, playing the dozens and boasting of sexual exploits with women.

Some men stood out above others in their work. One, a black man about forty years old, was referred to as the "iron man." He poured the hot molten iron from the huge brick-lined cast iron bucket into the rotating molding machines. He had thin features, a raspy voice, and moved with a slow gait and a cigarette hanging from his lips. The condition of his job required him to wear dark glasses to protect his eyes from the white glare of the hot molten iron. His clothing was protected by a heavy leather apron and leather leg pads that extended to the top of his work shoes to protect him from the occasional spillage of hot molten iron. At break time, the "iron man" would slip away into the filthy locker room area for a shot of liquor to calm his nerves from the stress of hard work. This was the work life of men in the foundries of the industrial North.

Once the men of my work crew discovered that I was college student, they encouraged me to stay in college and acquire an education to escape the demeaning work of the foundry system.

I was elated when summer ended and the dismissal whistle blew to end my last day of work. I, like Ishmael of Moby Dick, had escaped the dirty and smoke-filled belly of the "hell fire dungeon hole".

Me, Scholar/Athlete at Muskegon Heights High

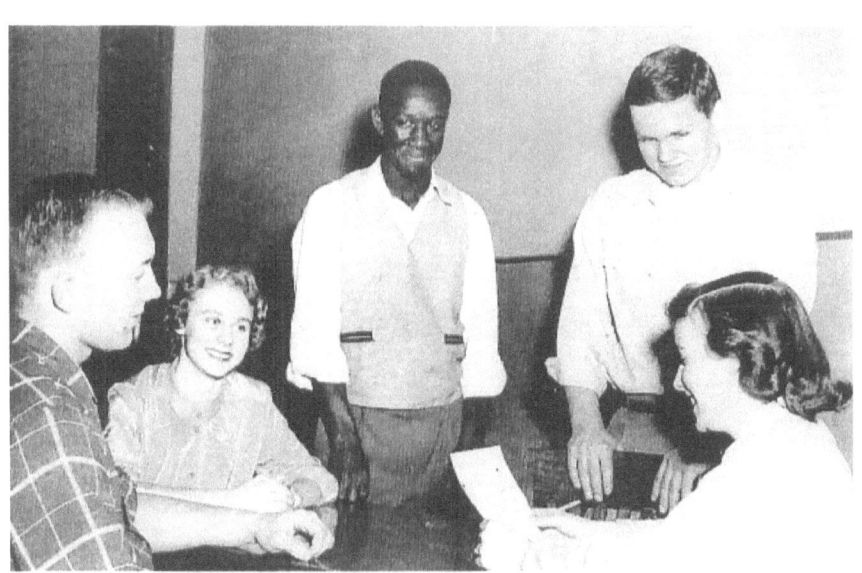

MUSKEGON HEIGHTS HIGH CLASS OFFICERS : 1953
From left to right: Arnold Ochs, Sergeant-at-arm, Janice Hawley/
Garber, Treasurer, Roy Phillips, Vice-President, James Davies,
President, Dorothy Hesselink/Vanderwert, Secretary

Vira Goosby-Phillips and Parents

Vira at Graduation 1957

Vira's Father Pierce Goosby

(1896-1984)

Vira's Mother Willie Mae

McGraw/Goosby (1910-1964)

Vira's Grandmother Octavia
Paschal/Goosby (1880-1970s)

CHAPTER EIGHT

A First In The Family

My acceptance at Eastern Michigan University, which was called Michigan State Normal School for teachers prior to 1957, was a time of deep reflection regarding how far the family had come. I had stood on the shoulders of ancestors who had risen above the storm of slavery, Reconstruction and Jim Crow segregation. The torch of the ancestors had been passed on to me to empower others along the way.

* * *

The day of departure arrived during the fall of 1954. This was the first time that I would be away from home, and it did not appear to be real. Mama had prepared the traditional travel meal of pound cake and fried chicken, which she placed in a shoe box.

I embraced Mama, Grandma and my girlfriend Vira after which my meager belongings were loaded into the trunk of the pastor's car. Dad and the Rev. Ward Stewart drove for approximately five hours to the town of Ypsilanti, located between Ann Arbor and Detroit. It was here that I would spend three years of my life.

I was assigned to Munson Hall, one of the men's residence halls. As many as four students were assigned to a suite, with a bedroom furnished with two double decked-beds, a dresser and two closets. A second room served as a study area, with desks and chairs. A shared bathroom with showers, sinks and toilets was located in the hallway on each of the three floors.

Most of the students came from Detroit, the city's suburbs and the Flint/Saginaw/Bay City area. Black students were assigned together and whites were assigned similarly. The foreign students, mainly from Middle Eastern, Asian, South American and African countries, generally were assigned with students from their own countries. Occasionally, Japanese were assigned with American white students.

The stigma of race was embedded in the cultural and social fabric of the college and small-town community. Small, quiet, sleepy and conservative, Ypsilanti was seven miles from Ann Arbor and approximately thirty miles from the Motor City. The town attracted a blue-collar workforce from the presence of a Ford Motor assembly plant and the Willow Run Airport. The area outside of the city was rural, which attracted a sizable southern white population, mainly from Kentucky and Tennessee. The campus climate reflected the racial attitudes of the town. There were no black professors or other black professionals on the campus. The only black worker was a custodian who served as a deacon at the local First Missionary Baptist Church, where I became a member.

After unpacking my clothing and choosing the area in the apartment that I would occupy, I was quickly drawn to a young man who entered the room. He had a broad, friendly smile on his face. He introduced himself as Robert Penn and our friendship began.

He was from Inkster, Michigan, a small suburban community of Detroit built by Henry Ford for black workers recruited from the South to work in his foundries and auto assembly plants. My roomie's career interest was in medicine. He was loquacious and outgoing. We spent the day and evening talking about our dreams upon graduation.

A few days later, another roommate, Aloysious M. Eaglin, arrived. He was a returning Korean War veteran who grew up in Opelousas, Louisiana. Older and serious, he was chemistry major. Milton Robinson, a New York physical education major who ran track, became our third roommate.

78

Social life on the campus was set by the various but segregated fraternities and sororities. Most of the white students had never experienced social relations with blacks. Their limited experiences were what they had heard through the media or had been taught through secondary sources. As a consequence, some white students carried stereotypical views and myths that focused on sex and interracial dating - a campus and community taboo.

These views were more relaxed on the larger University of Michigan campus in Ann Arbor. My intellectual seriousness and excellent study and note-taking habits caused students to seek me out for study, especially around examination time. This was especially the case with foreign students and white female classmates.

It was in my animal physiology class in 1956 that the only white female student in the class came across the room and selected me as her laboratory partner. We spent time studying together in the lounge of her dormitory. My coming to her residence drew strange and curious stares from other students, especially the dorm mothers of the residence hall.

Mama had cautioned me at an early age to never become involved with white women. Black mothers during this period were especially protective of their sons. They knew of the demise of Emmet Till, a black teenager from Chicago who was lynched for allegedly winking at a white woman during his visit with relatives in Mississippi in 1955. Black women feared similar circumstances for their sons. We were both aware of these social conditions, but our religious convictions gave us the strength and courage to become friends. She was a member of the Church of Jesus Christ of the Latter Day Saints, a branch of the Mormon faith. Her parents, missionary workers, had taken African students into their home. She had been shielded against any racial animosities toward blacks.

One Saturday evening, we decided to have a movie date in downtown Ann Arbor. After the movie, as we walked to the car, a carload of white guys stopped their car and pulled to the curb and began harassing us. "You white slut trash. We ain't good enough for you?" I became very upset and moved toward them. She grabbed my arm and restrained me. With a soft voice, she said, "Roy, don't waste your time."

I reflected upon what she said. They did not perceive us as just friends. They could only see us as sex partners. They saw a blue-eyed, strawberry blonde with a handsome black male.

Despite that and other experiences, we continued to be friends well into our married adult life. In fact, during our senior year, we student taught together at the college's Teaching School Laboratory.

My senior year brought serious changes in my life. I did not have enough money to cover my dormitory fees. I joined my two best friends, James Jackson and John McAdoo, and moved off campus. James was from Inkster and was studying to become a teacher. He came from a large family that had migrated from the South to work in the Ford Motor Auto Assembly plant. He had obtained an evening job at the Ypsilanti Ford plant while he attended college by day. With his earnings, he purchased a car, which made it possible for us to drive back and forth to school each day.

John, my other best friend, was from Detroit and the product of an interracial marriage. His mother was a Russian Jew and his father was a Black American who worked in the auto assembly plant. John was studying to become an educational psychologist. He had difficulty each day commuting from Detroit. When the weather was bad, we made a place for him in our dorm room before moving off campus.

We first moved into the home of a Jamaican widow who rented us two upstairs rooms. She was still using wood for cooking and heating. There were no provisions to obtain heat in the upstairs rooms and we found it difficult to study in a room without heat during the cold winter months. We were forced to find another suitable location.

We were fortunate to find two rooms with another older lady who lived alone. Mrs. Williams permitted us the full use of her home, including the kitchen to prepare our meals. She was a mother away from home. During the weekend, she would rise early to prepare our meals before going to work.

I worked two part-time jobs to earn enough to cover my college expenses. I maintained a job at the college cafeteria and a second one as an orderly at the University of Michigan Hospital on the weekends. Each Saturday and Sunday, I hitchhiked a ride to and from the hospital. There was no difficulty in obtaining a ride since people of the area were friendly and understanding of college students earning their way through college.

Since one of my roommates also worked at the hospital, we decided to search for a residence in Ann Arbor and used our other roommate's car to drive to the campus in Ypsilanti. We were fortunate to find a residence with an older couple, Mr. and Mrs. Elmer Knox, who rented us their basement apartment.

We had moved up a notch, having a private entrance, a bedroom, a kitchen and study social area. We pooled our funds to pay the rent and buy food. We shared housekeeping responsibilities. I was enjoying the independence of manhood

On my twenty-first birthday, two friends took me out on the town to a favorite beer pub, the Pretzel Bell in downtown Ann Arbor. They challenged me to a beer drinking contest as the college rite to manhood. I did not realize the impact of beer drinking since I did not indulge in college drinking. Before the evening had ended, I had consumed at least five large pitchers of beer! The impact did not hit me until I attempted to fall asleep. My head went into a tailspin, stomach pains began to come in cycles, and gushes of half-digested food spewed from my mouth. I had never felt this sick before. I made a steady path to the bathroom to empty my stomach of its contents.

The next morning, which was Sunday, my head was aching. I then understood what was meant by a "hangover." When I came to my senses, I vowed to myself that this would never happen again, not ever during my lifetime.

Graduation time was nearing. I prepared my employment credentials and began to search for teaching opportunities. I had completed my student teaching requirements in secondary science education with emphasis in the biological sciences with a near 3.0 average. I perceived that I was ready for hire since there was a demand for science teachers across the nation. I was in for a big surprise. I made it a point to seek interviews with as many school districts as possible.

One day, my former high school economics teacher, who had encouraged me to pursue teaching as a career, appeared on campus to interview prospective new teachers for the Muskegon Heights School District. I signed up for an interview. I had been one of the top graduates from the high school, achieving the highest scholastic and athletic honors as well as obtaining an "A" in his class.

Upon entering the interview, we shook hands and exchanged pleasantries. I perceived a nervous twitch on his face. He feigned a false smile and tried to crack a few jokes. "How are you doing, Roy?" he asked. Before I could respond, he cut it short and said, "You know, Roy, we would like to have a good colored teacher in the school district, but some members of our community are not ready for us to have a colored yet." Before he said another word, I stood abruptly, shook his hand and thanked him for the interview.

I understood but did not accept his fear of hiring a popular black male high school alumnus. I remembered an incident that happened during the noon hour in the school halls one day during my senior year in high school. I was standing near my locker having a friendly conversation with a white female. When he passed by us, his face turned reddish with a displeasing frown on his brow.

I realized at this moment in my life that it was not my educational achievements that counted. Rather, it was the perception and fear of my black male sexual credentials that made the difference in the mind of some personnel recruiters.

The words of Big Mama and my father flashed before me as I left the interview: "When you find that you have given it your best shot and do not succeed, do not become bitter or angry, move on to your next challenge." I did just that.

I interviewed with other public schools within the Detroit metropolitan area and met the same reservation. I decided to apply for graduate school to move myself to another level of credentialing. I was accepted as a graduate student at the Horace H. Rackham School of Graduate Studies at the University of Michigan to pursue a master's degree in the biological sciences.

At this time, Uncle Sam was knocking at my door for induction into the armed services. The Korean conflict had ended, but the Cold War with Russia had reached a potential point of conflict. I passed my physical examination. I had taken two years of ROTC training at Eastern Michigan and this had qualified me for officer candidacy. My brother was serving in the Air Force in Germany. At the last moment, I received a letter from the Selective Services Board System notifying me of a deferment to attend graduate school.

In the meantime, my girlfriend Vira had graduated from high school and decided to move to Flint to live with her sister and brother-in-law to seek employment. After an unsuccessful search for employment there, I proposed to her. She consented, even though we had not announced this important decision to our parents. During the last weekend in July 1957, we boarded a Greyhound bus in Flint and headed for a new beginning in Ann Arbor. We had no money and little clothing, but we had each other.

My roommates agreed to give up the apartment that we shared to make it possible for Vira and me to begin a new life together. We exchanged vows on August 5, 1957, at the Washtenaw Courthouse in Ann Arbor.

I had obtained a full-time job as an orderly at the University of Michigan Hospital on the afternoon shift, while attending graduate school during the day. Vira obtained employment at the veteran's hospital as a secretary, but had to quit due to early morning sickness.

With a baby on the way, I had to begin planning for a teaching career to supplement my income for a new family. I circulated my teaching credentials from the placement office of the University of Michigan. I immediately was offered a position at the Pontiac and the Detroit public schools. I accepted the offer for a higher salary and an opportunity to teach biology and general mathematics at Central High School on the west side of Detroit.

Uncle Sam sent me a second notice to report for induction. I immediately forwarded a letter to the Selective Services Board, advising it of my marital status and the expectancy of becoming a father. I received a second and final deferment from serving in the armed services. We began preparing for my new teaching career with the Detroit Public Schools.

CHAPTER NINE

The Tumultuous Sixties And Seventies

The decades of the sixties and seventies represented rapid and tumultuous change. The period was the beginning of the racial maturation of America. The legal walls of segregation in housing, voting, public accommodation, employment and education imposed during the period following Reconstruction began to crumble. The central cities of urban America exploded in rebellion. The Civil Rights Movement climaxed with the assassinations of President John Kennedy, Martin Luther King Jr., Bobby Kennedy, Medgar Evers and Malcolm X; the American military industrial complex became involved in an unpopular war in the jungles of Vietnam; a segment of the nation's youth rose up in rebellion against what some perceived as an increasing materialistic culture that left a large segment of its population in poverty; a youth drug culture emerged and a "me" generation was spawned; a feminist movement emerged on the tail of a declining affirmative action agenda as women and an emerging Hispanic, immigrant ethnic group began to take center stage in America.

* * *

The beginning of my professional career also was the beginning of my new family - the fifth generation after slavery.

When Vira and I moved to Detroit to begin my new teaching career, the Motor City was undergoing major changes. Automation was rapidly moving into the workplace and a new information service-based society was emerging. Employment downsizing was becoming the buzzword in the manufacturing and smokestack industries of the North, Midwest and Northeast.

My ticket into the teaching profession came as the Detroit public schools' demographic profile was changing from predominantly white to black. This phenomenon accelerated the white middle class' flight to the suburbs, made possible by the extension of the metropolitan expressway system that radiated like spokes of a wheel from the center of the city to its outer fringes. Downtown merchants and the industrial establishment joined the exodus, making it difficult for central city residents to access opportunities in an emerging service-based economy. The slow pace of upward mobility among a segment of blacks into first-, middle- and senior-line management positions within the public and private sectors of the workforce gave rise to a higher level of expectation for change. This consciousness became the focus of a national civil rights movement, which became emboldened by the agenda of black college student leaders, primarily in the Southeast. The movement later spread to predominantly white colleges in the North, West and East.

The national movement focused on equal access and opportunity for blacks in employment, housing, education, public accommodations, criminal justice, voting and political representation.

Black leadership captured and mobilized the mood of this rising black consciousness. The resulting effect was the shedding of the racial designation of "Colored" and "Negro" designated by our slave masters. We named ourselves "Black" and "African American."

While numerous leaders emerged to represent the various factions of the movement, Dr. Martin Luther King, Jr., who led the Montgomery, Alabama, bus boycott, emerged as the movement's premier spokesman. King's strategy during the early stages of the movement was devoted primarily to public accommodation and voting rights, buoyed by a successful coalition with key white leadership within the labor and religious communities.

During the first three years of our marriage, Vira and I brought three lovely children into our lives. Our first child was born April 29, 1958, and we named him Roy Jr. His birth coincided with the passing of Grandma Sarah Chatman/Wilson/Cook, who died in her sleep at the age of 95. She was born two years before the end of slavery.

Vira and I drove home to Muskegon Heights and paid our last respects to this pioneer who had purchased land with funds from the Freedman's Bureau during the period of Reconstruction. Her remains were shipped home to the small farming community of Longview near Benton, Louisiana.

The following year on March 6, 1959, we had another boy, whom we named Kevin Darryl. He was born on the anniversary death of his grandmother, Mary Jane, who had passed away sixteen years earlier.

Vira devoted herself to the caring and nurturing of our two sons. We decided that she would remain at home during the children's early years. Each day I was eager to arrive home from my teaching assignment to hear of the children's new experiences.

Each summer beginning in 1959, I took advantage of National Science Fellowships to attend workshops at various colleges and universities including Western Michigan, Indiana University, Cornell and Wayne State universities. In 1957, the Russians placed the first satellite, Sputnik, into space, spurring a national concern about the numbers of science educators, scientists and engineers. It was my intent to have impressive credentials.

After the summer of the 1959 National Science Fellowship Institute at Western Michigan University in Kalamazoo, Vira and I decided to load the two boys and one of her sisters, Vernell, into our newly purchased 1954 Ford and return to our southern roots to visit our relatives in Louisiana and Arkansas.

Southern states were resisting the move from legal segregation to desegregation, and I had been advised to drive without stopping for accommodations since many of the small motels and restaurants had not opened their doors to black consumers. We only stopped for gas and milk for the boys.

The Klansmen were active in spotting automobile tags with out-of-state licenses. Many students from northern colleges and universities were heading south to assist black citizens in voter registration and marches. We did not encounter any negative incidents along the way. In fact, the whites we encountered appeared friendly and accommodating. Many of the small communities along the route were struggling economically and appeared eager to accept the dollars of passing tourists, regardless of their race.

We were greatly relieved when we reached the town of Cullen/ Springhill. Aunt Ruthann, Uncle Leamon and their daughter Lola Mae were excited to see us. After being introduced to my family, Aunt Ruthann looked me up and down and shouted out in excitement, "Little Joe! Boy you sho' look like yo' Mama, Mae Jane." Aunt Ruthann was my natural Mama's sister.

Aunt Ruthann prepared a special southern meal of turnip greens, corn bread, black-eyed peas, fried chicken, peach cobbler and lemonade. Afterward, we spent the evening catching up and reminiscing.

"Do you 'member yo' Mama, Mae Jane?" Aunt Ruthann asked. "I sho do 'member her. She wanted Webb and me to continue our schooling, grow up and become good men. She really would be proud of us," I said.

The small town of Cullen/Springhill was not the busy and bustling town I knew as a child. Only one black grocery and hardware, both owned by the Rhones, remained. Along the main road through Froggy Bottom, many black business establishments stood closed and boarded up.

Many of my old school mates had left the area for better opportunities up North and out West. Those who remained were standing idle along the red dirt road, leaning on their pick-up and pulp wood trucks with bottles of beer and whiskey in their hands. I could not recognize them. Their eyes were blood shot from drinking bad whiskey and living the hard life of southern rural black men. They had withered away in the past, the surplus labor force and increasing underclass of the rural South.

Like many of the black women of her generation, Aunt Ruthann was still industrious and full of life. She had built a new home, saved her money, raised and college educated her only child. She had been injured at work at the paper mill and, as a result, placed on disability. She had used her disability and retirement earnings to manage a small restaurant and beauty salon.

The old three-room school building that I had attended had been closed and converted into a service center. A new high school for black students had been built at Springhill. It was to be short-lived since the talk of desegregating the schools was under way.

Mama Caroline heard that I was home. She was now eighty years old and eager to see her deceased daughter's baby boy. She sent her two sons to come and take us to her old farm in Growing Valley. When we arrived, she and her husband, Mister Green, were sitting on the front porch as was the tradition of southern black folks during the summer evening hours.

When Mama Caroline saw us approaching, she ran to embrace us. She had not seen me since my childhood. She shouted out, "Little Joe, Mae Jane's boy!" I'm so glad to see y'all." I was excited to see her well in her old age. She stood tall and straight as I had remembered her during my childhood. She had labored many years behind a mule, plowing the fields, picking cotton and raising her children, and now her grandchildren. Some of her children of failed marriages had sent their children home to be reared by her, an increasing social occurrence in the family's history.

"Y'all come on in. I cooked some fried chicken, greens and candied yams," Mama Caroline said. This brought back fond memories of a hearty meal served after working long hours in the hot fields.

The land around the old wooden shanty was lying fallow. There were no longer rows of cotton, corn, sugar cane, yams or peanuts to harvest. My grandparents had grown too old to farm. The land was overgrown with sprawling weeds, bushes and small sprouting trees. The old barn behind the house provided shelter for an old mule that had outlived its usefulness. The offspring had left the land to work in the factories of urban America.

A few pigs and chickens wandered about in the open field area in search of food. When evening approached, I thought of the toils and struggles of the slave ancestors and their children who had worked hard to make a better future for their offspring.

We sat on the front porch and watched the full moon rise on the eastern horizon above the forest canopy. The moonlight shone brightly and the nocturnal creatures came out of their nests and hiding places. Little lightning bugs appeared with their shining lights as small flickering flashes in the night. The call of the whippoorwill and singing of the katydids and crickets filled the night air. This was the old South I had known as a child.

The next few days we visited with other relatives and went by the old church and school, which had been torn down. A new brick church had been erected near the school site. The church cornerstone was still legible with its inscription of the founding minister and deacons. The Rev. Jessie Dixon was still the pastor of the church.

The time was approaching for us to bid farewell. We headed for the Arkansas line to see Vira's relatives. Her sister and grandmother still lived on their 300-acre farm near the city of Magnolia, Arkansas. They were glad to see Vira who had grown into a fine young woman, now with her own family. After a few days of visiting, we headed home to the Motor City where other changes in the family began to occur.

The beginning of the 1960s brought a beautiful little girl into the family. She was born on February 16, 1960. We named her Crystal. She was the first child in our family to be born in a racially integrated hospital. White hospitals in Detroit began to accept black doctors on their staff for the first time during this period.

The children were taught our traditional values of caring for one another and developing a love for learning. They were christened at the St. Andrews Presbyterian Church. We exposed them to art, music, science and technology to prepare them for school as Big Mama and our parents had taught us. Weekends and holidays were spent visiting the zoo, a recreation park called Belle Isle, and the Museum of Natural History at the University of Michigan.

The family had grown to the point where we needed a home of our own. The children needed space to run and play in a safe environment. Middle-income professional black families were moving westward in the Six and Seven Mile and Outer Drive areas of the city. Blacks tended to follow the Jewish migration to the western suburbs of Oak Park and Southfield. We moved into a quiet, all white neighborhood, but in just a short time, other blacks began to purchase homes in the area.

By 1964, I had earned my master's degree in science education from Wayne State University. This opened opportunities for me to teach biology and physical science at Northern High School, an inner city school in Detroit, where Dr. King visited in 1965.

After Dr. King's visit, the students mobilized against the new, unpopular white principal who had placed a police officer within the school to assist in the enforcement of the truancy policy. The police officer was a huge, strapping black man with crude mannerisms. He had a tendency of disciplining students in public, grabbing their clothing and marching them from the streets into the building. His behavior bordered on brutality. A small core of the student leaders organized and demanded the removal of the policeman and principal.

The students organized a successful walkout and boycotted until the school superintendent removed the principal to a downtown desk job. The policeman was also removed A black principal was put into place. This unprecedented action soon spread to other central city schools within the city and eventually to other all-black schools throughout the nation.

The Detroit Public School Board had become pro labor, black and Jewish. This new composition permitted black citizens a forum to appear before the board to address their grievances. Subsequently, a group of black ministers and labor leaders formed a coalition of concerned citizens who approached the board, demanding a greater presence of black construction apprentices and tradesmen on school building projects. The school system operated two trade schools, one in construction trades training and the other in the preparation of apprentices in the automotive manufacturing trades. Responding to the coalition's demands, the school board authorized two administrative positions to enforce a newly created policy on affirmative action with vendors and labor unions doing business with the public school system.

While I had no experience in negotiating with contractors and labor unions in this new emerging area, I applied for the affirmative action position, which was designed to crack racial barriers within the tough construction trades and labor unions. I was interviewed and was successful in being appointed to the position, the first affirmative action program of its kind in a public school system.

The school system had a capital budget of approximately $200 million for construction, remodeling and school repairs. The new policy required all school vendors and contractors bidding on school board contracts to develop a program of equal employment opportunity in hiring, transfer and promotion of its employees regardless of race, color, creed or national origin.

The job of the affirmative action officers was to visit, audit and assist firms to develop nondiscriminatory employment policies, programs and practices in their company's workforce. If firms failed to show positive results over a period of time, they were given notice of noncompliance and were required to establish employment goals and timetables to achieve results as job openings and promotional opportunities became available.

Companies and labor unions that made no attempts to be fair were placed on a list for possible non renewal of their contracts during the next round of bidding for work.

Since I had no experience in this area, I took the initiative to seek education and professional training. Luckily, I was acquainted with Walter Greene, a church member who was employed as a high-level governmental official with affirmative action compliance responsibilities within the Federal Office of Contract Compliance. His office had compliance oversight of the automotive giants: General Motors, Ford, Chrysler and their associated labor unions. He became my mentor and taught me the knowledge and skills of the job.

I accompanied him in a compliance visit with the big brass at General Motors, the No. 1 auto corporate giant in the world at that time. In his quarterly compliance report of the corporation's EEO record, Walter noted some progress in the hiring of blacks, primarily in the semi-skilled assembly workforce, but very little or no progress in the skilled trades, technical and management areas of the organization.

We made an inspection tour of the workforce where black workers were fairly well represented within the unskilled section of assembly line work. As we proceeded to cleaner and more technical areas of the plant, the workforce became whiter.

I asked my mentor, "Why is there such a noticeable absence of blacks in the skilled trades?" He replied, "Most of the skilled tradesmen are trained, recruited and hired from apprentices within the manufacturing and construction trade schools operated by the Detroit Public Schools."

Furthermore, he said, "boys tend to follow their fathers' occupations in the blue collar trades." The joint management labor committees that governed the operation of these trades had a long history of excluding blacks. This was the challenge for change.

My first task was an assessment of all of the apprenticeship and vocational technical programs that the school system had to offer. A racial ethnic profile was made of each program to determine the potential pool of black students for recruitment and orientation into job career opportunities offered in the construction and automotive industry. Prior to each high school graduation period, letters were forwarded to black high school graduates to interest them in further training opportunities in the skilled trades.

The merger of the office of contract compliance with the office of guidance added a new staff member and two secretaries. The new staff member was an elder black administrator, Ernest T. Marshal, who had a long history of assisting black students to obtain employment with companies within the Detroit metropolitan community.

Our combined effort resulted in new opportunities for black students in the construction trades of metropolitan Detroit. Marshal and I negotiated the placement of black male apprentices into trades that had been closed to blacks, including plumbing, pipefitting, electrical, iron work, sprinkler fitting, sheet metal and elevator work.

While there was a rising level of expectation for accelerated socio-economic improvements in education and other areas of employment, conflicts between the predominantly all white Detroit Police Department with segments of the inner city Detroit community erupted in widespread street violence during the evening of July 23, 1967.

I stood on the second floor balcony of my west side home and observed billows of black smoke rising from an area approximately five miles away. A few minutes later, a news bulletin flashed across the TV screen announcing that a disturbance was in progress along 12th and 14th avenues in Detroit's west central black business district.

It was reported that an all-white police unit had attempted to close down a "blind pig" along 12th Avenue. The area, a typical street found in most black inner city communities, was filled with liquor stores, bars, pawn shops, low-credit furniture and clothing stores, barbershops, beauty parlors, numbers joints and houses of prostitution. It was "Froggy Bottom" up north, except most of the businesses were white-owned, primarily by white Jewish merchants.

The scene of the disturbance depicted blacks being handcuffed and paraded into police units and hauled away to downtown police headquarters to be booked and jailed. The scene attracted crowds of angry bystanders who protested and shouted out angry remarks of "police brutality." The city already had undergone the profiling of some prominent black males, which had created tension between the police and segments of the black community.

The crowd near the scene quickly became unruly and began throwing bottles and Molotov cocktails into unattended stores. Then the mob turned over and fire bombed unoccupied police cars.

The lawless elements of the streets took over and the crowd rushed into liquor, clothing and furniture stores removing all properties not bolted down. After widespread looting, stores were set on fire causing fires to spread quickly into surrounding areas.

The area quickly became a war zone. The police and fire departments were unprepared to handle the escalating disturbance. Gunshots from the police and lawless elements added to the confusion and violence. Additional police and fire units streamed in and cordoned off the impacted area.

Law-abiding citizens joined with business owners and armed themselves to protect the remains of their properties. Innocent whites passing through the area were caught up in the melee and attacked by street hoodlums shouting out racial slurs, "Whiteys and pigs, git out of our community."

Shortly after midnight, the police gained control of the area. The mayor established a citywide curfew, prohibiting all movement, except for authorized personnel. A state of emergency was declared by the governor. The National Guard and special units of the military were called in for assistance.

The 1967 Detroit rebellion represented a turning point in race relations within the city and the nation. A white backlash directed against affirmative action programs designed to address the historical grievances of blacks in employment, economics, housing, education, political representation and police-community relations began to wane from the national consciousness.

The aftermath of the Detroit Rebellion led to the creation of a biracial blue ribbon committee, The New Detroit Committee. Its primary focus was to develop a plan for revitalization and to establish a positive climate to address long-standing racial grievances.

Similarly, the federal government established the Kerner Commission to study the issues and conditions leading to urban rebellions and to make appropriate recommendations for improvements. Some of the recommendations resulted in the initiation of the Great Society Program under the leadership of President Lyndon Johnson. However, the political mood of the country shifted toward a more conservative approach under President Nixon.

Major universities and corporations began to establish educational leadership and management training programs to recruit blacks into positions of management. Realizing that I had to be two steps ahead of the game to position myself for emerging opportunities, I applied and was accepted into an educational doctoral program at the University of Michigan. The university had established a National Educational Leadership Program in partnership with the Charles Stewart Mott Foundation and Flint Public Schools. This program afforded me an opportunity to receive a fellowship that would pay living expenses to move my young family to Flint as a university resident intern within the Flint Public Schools. Under this arrangement, I was able to finish my graduate course work at the Michigan campus in Ann Arbor. The Detroit Public Schools granted me a year's sabbatical leave. Vira and I placed our home in the care of her two younger sisters and their families. We moved to Flint in September of 1967.

Like Detroit, Flint is an automotive manufacturing city focusing primarily in the production of General Motors auto products - Chevrolets and Buicks. It was a blue-collar town, attracting many southern blacks and whites as well as southeastern European ethnic groups. Each group lived in its separate small neighborhood enclaves.

We rented an apartment on the outer fringes of the city and enrolled our three children at the Steward Elementary School. Vira spent her time attending the children and revisiting family members who had moved from Muskegon Heights to work in the booming automotive industry.

In addition to my assigned school internship, I joined my peers within the graduate leadership program in the short drive to the University of Michigan campus at Ann Arbor to finish my required doctoral course work.

The Michigan campus was an exciting place to be during this period. Graduate and undergraduate students were actively engaged in the great political debates of the decade including the Vietnam conflict and civil rights.

Racial tensions were especially high following the assassination of Malcolm X in 1963 and Dr. Martin Luther King, Jr. in 1968. These two events witnessed a turn in the Civil Rights Movement's emphasis from the moral issues that had previously held together a coalition of moderate groups. A white backlash began to emerge regarding affirmative action.

These issues were played out in the streets, debated in the hallways of Congress and the classrooms of academia. Many of my white graduate peers were from small mid-western and southern towns. They had very little social contacts with educated blacks. They needed to be sensitized to the issues of race within the American society.

To accomplish this task, each week seminars were scheduled that attracted national speakers to address broad issues impacting the policy decisions facing school leaders within large urban school districts. Alex Haley was one of the lecturers.

By the end of the spring 1969 term, I had successfully passed my preliminary examination and completed all doctoral course requirements. While all of this was happening, Vira announced that our fourth child was on the way.

It was a girl born at the Flint Hurley Hospital on Mother's Day, May 11, 1969. We named her Kelley Tremelle. Our second daughter was a spitting image of her oldest sister Crystal who had been born nine years earlier. Vira and I agreed that this was enough for us to support and educate.

Since my residential requirements had been completed, we returned to Detroit. For my dissertation, I had an interest in researching equal opportunity in one of the Detroit metropolitan building trades. I was especially interested in researching the attitudes of white apprentices, the future workforce of the industry, with respect to their attitudes regarding affirmative action. I had developed good relations with the new, young business manager of the local pipe fitters union. He and his predecessor also had an interest in the topic.

The pipe fitting industry in the Metropolitan Detroit area and the Detroit Public Schools gave me permission to proceed with my idea. My doctoral committee also approved the research proposal for the study. I was well on my way to conducting the research when Aubrey McCutcheon, the deputy superintendent for Labor and Personnel Relations, recommended me for the position of assistant principal at one of the troubled junior high schools.

A group of parents and community activists in the Miller Junior High feeder pattern requested my appointment as assistant principal. The Miller Junior High School Council was chaired by a very articulate black female, Mrs. Anna McDonald. I had taught her son in my former role as science teacher at Miller approximately ten years earlier.

At the time of the appointment, I was 35, highly energetic, visionary, risk taking and committed to quality improvement of student learning, and parent and teacher participation in a shared model of school governance.

The principal was an older white female, Miss Edith Edwards, whom I had known as a physical education teacher from an earlier assignment. She was nearing retirement and needed an effective assistant principal who could establish effective relationships with students, parents and faculty. The former assistant principal had been a black male, who ran afoul with the black parents regarding his manner of discipline with students. Because of her frequent absence from the school, she delegated the daily running of the school to me.

The school was undergoing a transition from a predominantly black school to one of racial diversity. The city's urban renewal program started in the early sixties had resulted in the construction of new town houses, a new shopping center, upscale restaurants and a new innovative school – Chrysler Elementary - that was attracting young white and black professionals from the suburbs into the downtown community. Historically, the area had been black and poor. The new parents were highly educated, affluent and demanded better schools and safe neighborhoods. They also wanted to improve the nearby middle and junior high school where their children could attend.

My first leadership challenge occurred at a student assembly, which had been arranged by a group of black students who had received approval from the principal to invite a black high school student to address the student body. The principal and school community agent, the Rev. James Wadsworth, had not discussed the nature of the assembly with me.

The president of the student council introduced the speaker, a student at Martin Luther King High School. When the student began talking, it was obvious that he did not have his speech together. He began to mumble his words, "I...I jest wanna say right on to all y'all, brothers and sisters," he said as he held up his fist in the black power salute. He took a long pause before speaking again.

He shouted out in an angry, defiant tone, "I want all y'all white folks to leave the auditorium 'cause my message today is to black people." A few of the student revolutionary types, wearing their Black Panther jackets, stood and shouted "Right on."

Since the principal was absent that day, the teachers in the audience looked around at me standing by the door to end this nonsense. I seized the moment and approached the podium and kindly asked the student to remove himself. He obeyed with a look of confusion on his face. At that moment, pandemonium broke out as some of the more vocal and militant students in the crowd rose in protest, demanding that I allow the student to finish his speech. I raised my hand to calm the crowd and announced in a clear tone of voice, "Students, I am sorry, but this part of the assembly has ended."

I utilized the opportunity to teach a lesson and to dialogue with the students concerning the consequences of this action. I apologized to the students and teachers regarding the quick manner in which the assembly had been organized. I also thanked the young man for his time and effort. I did not wish to further embarrass and put him down in front of his friends and peers.

I said in a very authoritative manner, "Students and faculty, I began my teaching career here at Miller. It is an honor to be back here to assist in making Miller a model for excellence in teaching and learning. I need your help in making this happen. Our first order of business is working together and respecting each other as a team. All of the teachers in this room must be respected. They came here to teach. They are not responsible for what happened in the past, but they are responsible for assisting you in not making the same mistakes we have learned from our history. I will tell you that all of us should be equally angry at our own people who assisted in selling our ancestors into slavery. In fact, a few white men in a ship could not have gone into the bush country of Africa without the cooperation of chiefs and others in control of our people. This is a new day, where we must work together to make positive changes in our school. Let me see the hands of those students who are willing to help."

Many students raised their hand. A black male student who had indicated membership in the Black Panther Party came forth. "Mr. Phillips, I would like to see black history taught in the school," he said.

The president of the student council said, "We need to create a mural of black history on the wall in the front halls and paint all the lockers red, green and black to symbolize the black nationalist flag."

A white female student shouted out from the back of the auditorium: "I would like to see a new cafeteria and a change in the school schedule to allow students to have club activities to make our school a more enjoyable place to be."

The assembly was dismissed on a good note and I requested the student leaders to meet with me in my office.

After a few minutes of dialoguing with the students, a group of students rushed into the office and frantically announced, "Mr.

Phillips, a white teacher referred to us as 'niggers'!" They loudly demanded, "What are you going to do about it?"

The situation had become grave. I sent the lead counselor to take over the teacher's class and requested that the teacher report to my office. The accused teacher was a small white man who had previous difficulties teaching his class. I informed the teacher of the charges that students had brought against him. I requested that he provide me with his version of what had happened in his class. He was very nervous and apologetic and said, "I may have used the wrong words in describing how the students had behaved in the auditorium, but I had no intent in being derogatory."

I told him that he had to be removed from the school for his own safety since some of the more militant students in the school might attempt to cause him harm and I did not wish to see that happen. My supervisor, the region superintendent, was informed of the incident. I requested that the teacher be placed at another school and he consented.

After that action, the word went out from the students that the new assistant principal did not take any "shit" from racist teachers or unruly students who wanted to take over the school.

I informed the principal of what had happened upon her return and offered recommendations for changing the climate of the school. She indicated full confidence in my leadership and to proceed with all deliberate speed in getting the job done. Before a plan was developed, the principal announced her retirement and the superintendent appointed me the principal of the school. I appointed Mr. Homer Pugh, a former school counselor, as my white assistant principal. We became a team to improve the school.

A six-point program that addressed the school community's concerns was implemented. Students took ownership and pride in their school. The hallways were clear of students between classes; the school attendance and punctuality improved drastically; expulsion and suspensions became nonexistent; school discipline problems were reduced; school graffiti was eliminated; and students developed a respect for themselves and authority figures

But despite major improvements within the school, the community was still surrounded by poverty. Drugs were entering the community and schools, and violence was on the increase, especially among teenagers in the schools. Angry young men who started their feuds in the neighborhood were ending them in the schools.

The school had been so peaceful, but there were storms brewing outside of its walls.

It was a quiet morning in the spring of 1971 when a group of students rushed into my office shouting out, "Dr. Phillips, Dr. Phillips, a girl has been stabbed in the basement hallway and she is lying on the floor in a pool of blood!" I shouted out to the staff, "My God! My God, call the police, emergency medical team and the girl's parents!"

I rushed to the scene of the incident as the police and emergency medical team were entering the building. The site was quickly cordoned off and students were removed from the scene. I jumped into the rear of the ambulance to accompany and console the student in route to the hospital. I watched her slowly lose her breath, and her eyes closed as the medical personnel attended her. She was pronounced dead upon arrival at the hospital.

I was stunned. My body became numb and tears streamed down my face. The only thought that crossed my mind was that a child had been killed in my school hallway. When I returned to school, students gathered in my office to tell me the story of what had happened. They provided the female student's name who had committed the terrible act. The two students lived next door to each other and had been friends; however, a feud had broken out between them over a boy in whom the two had a romantic interest. An argument had broken out in the victim's yard and the feud was brought to school where it ended in violence and fatality.

She was the second Miller student to die from a senseless killing. The first was a student who led a movement to place a black history mural in the front hall. He had been killed in the neighborhood by a security officer who alleged that he and his friend had broken into a lumberyard late one night. Now it was this child, killed at the hands of her friend.

* * *

During the summer of 1971, I had completed my research project for the Ph.D. degree. The family prepared to accompany me to the graduation exercise at the main campus of the University of Michigan in Ann Arbor. Dad and Mama came from Los Angeles to be with me and the family. They had provided the encouraging support to assist me in reaching this high point in my life. I looked around me and discovered that I was the only black male receiving this highest honor.

During the spring of 1972, two major opportunities became available for me. The Rockefeller Foundation selected me as an understudy to become a school superintendent. Wayne County Community College offered me the position of vice president for administration. After discussing the two options with Vira and the children, I accepted the challenge at Wayne County Community College.

CHAPTER TEN

A Career Within The American Community College System

The Civil Rights Movement sparked a racial maturation in the American psyche. The new spirit penetrated significant American institutions, including those in higher education, to open their doors to the disenfranchised. Leading this movement was the emerging community colleges that advanced an open-door policy for nontraditional students desiring to enroll in higher education.

My community college career extended nearly 30 years from 1972 until the end of 2001. My career took my family from Detroit to the cities of Seattle, Omaha and Miami, where I ended my tenure as the founding president of Miami-Dade Community College's Homestead Campus.

* * *

The challenge was to develop a new community college with campus facilities in the city and the out-county areas of the Detroit metropolitan Wayne County. It was one of the last urban metropolitan counties in the state without a comprehensive community college system.

The college was created by an act of the Michigan state legislature in 1969, two years after the Detroit rebellion. The college headquarters were established on Woodward Avenue within the central core of the city. The college's service area encompassed approximately two million residents. The city itself had undergone a major shift in its socio-economic profile from predominantly white to African American with a heavy concentration of urban poor.

The college was created without a major funding source. The voters of the county created a local Board of Trustees to set policy for the new college but failed to vote for a millage level to support the college operations and capital outlay needs. The urban college was forced to depend upon the political mood of a rural-dominated state legislature As a consequence, the college operated from student matriculation fees and a special state appropriation. The fast growth rate of the new institution and poor internal management caused the institution to go bankrupt during the initial years of its operation.

The doors of the college opened in the fall of 1969 with an expected enrollment of 2,000 students. Instead, more than 8,000 students showed up, eager to receive the first two years of higher education. The open-door admission policy permitted the enrollment of students 18 years or older with a high school diploma or GED. The college had no facilities of its own and, therefore, was required to lease facilities at more than 20 locations throughout the county in public and parochial high schools, churches, community centers, and a downtown YMCA.

After the college had suffered bankruptcy in the early '70s, its founding president was replaced with an interim president who was a well-respected black county fiscal executive. He was hired to get the finances of the college in shape prior to the hiring of a new president.

Dr. Reginald Wilson, a black educational psychologist, had gained his reputation as the founder and director of the Black Studies Program at Oakland Community College, located in Metropolitan Detroit's northern suburb. He was a scholar and one of the few black community college presidents of the 1970s who served as chief executive officer of an urban community college district.

Wilson delegated a great deal of the responsibilities for operating the college to his four senior management vice presidents: academic, administration, finance and student services. By 1975, I had assisted

Wilson and the team to develop a five-year facilities master plan and successfully lobby the state legislature to levy .25 mill over a five-year period to begin the building of five college campuses. The first $40 million was used to build three campuses, including two in the city and one in the out-county community.

I had achieved my professional goals and felt that I was ready to assume the role of a community college president. Vira had enrolled at the University of Michigan to continue her education. Roy Junior, Kevin and Crystal were enrolled at the prestigious Cass Technical High School. I had applied and became a serious candidate for a presidency within the Seattle Community College District to head its downtown central campus. I had reservations about leaving Detroit, and I had been offered a campus vice presidency at Florida Community College in Jacksonville. It took a family decision to relocate to another city, especially Seattle, a long way from the place of my professional roots.

When I made the announcement to Wilson, whom I had developed close working relationships, he was hesitant to see me pull up stakes, but he realized that my professional growth was ahead of me. In fact, he realized that there were only a few African-American community college presidents, and he viewed this as an opportunity to add to our numbers.

The presidency at Seattle Central Community College was a most difficult challenge. The day that I flew into the city, there was a snow storm and the plane could not land, causing the flight to be rerouted to Portland, Oregon. I thought of the storm as an omen.

I had accepted the position at Seattle without a careful study of the college's campus history and climate. Seattle Central Community College was the oldest of three campuses. One was located to service the North Seattle District and a new one was under construction in South Seattle, although students were attending classes in portable units. The Central Campus was where the college district had its beginning. Like most community colleges, the district was created out of the Seattle Public Schools during the early 1960s. Many of the college's first faculty was hired from the teaching ranks of the public school. Most of the public school faculty was white, so upon my arrival, I found an older, highly unionized, predominantly white faculty and administrative staff.

The campus had two previous African-American presidents who experienced short tenures before leaving for better positions. The campus was located near the black central district and thus carried an image of a minority campus, even though black, Asian and Hispanic students were not in the majority in the classrooms. However, their numbers were greater than those on the other two campuses in the suburban areas.

The district was headed by a middle-aged, white male president, George Corcoran, who had been promoted to his role by serving as the coordinator of the "Troika," a group of the three campus presidents who rotated as acting district president. This rotation had come to an end when I assumed the presidency of the Central Campus.

A few weeks into my administration, a campus security staff rushed into my office and told me that community activists were threatening to shut down the construction work of a new project on campus because of a lack of minority workers and contractors at the site. I immediately left my office and headed for the site, across from the administration building. The news media also had assembled. The activist group previously had threatened to close down a black church construction project of a well-respected minister within the Central District a week earlier.

Emotions were high as I entered the site. A news reporter walked up to me with his microphone and a camera projected into my face with a rapid volley of questions: "Mr. President, does the college have an affirmative action policy for engaging minority workers and contractors for working on this project? And what does the college plan to do to resolve this crisis?"

I appeared very calm since I had experienced similar crises in previous positions within the Detroit Public Schools. I informed the media and addressed the leader of the community activist group that the college was willing to meet with the leaders of the Minority Contractors Association and the general contractor of the project to negotiate terms that would be of mutual benefit to the parties of the dispute. I politely requested the leader of the group to meet with me in my office and direct his group away from the site so that the construction workers could continue their work. He consented.

When I entered my office, the phone was ringing off the hook from other media, wanting to know how the college would resolve the issue of non-minority participation on the project. I responded that the college would issue a press release detailing the manner in which the crisis would be resolved.

The young community activist and I dialogued. I wanted to allow him to air his grievances behind closed doors. I proposed to meet with him, leaders of the Minority Contractors Association, other key community leaders, and my administrative dean at the local Urban League office. Meanwhile, my administrative dean and I conferred with the district president and general contractor of the crisis and outlined a proposal for the resolution of the issue.

The following evening, my dean and I met with the Minority Contractors Association and other key community leaders and presented a proposal to engage a qualified minority subcontractor who had experience in excavation and hauling to start the next day on the project. The proposal was accepted by the leaders of the Minority Contractors Association.

The next day, a news release was issued by the college detailing a settlement. The settlement provided high community profile and visibility to the new central campus president. This positive media image would be short-lived.

Vira and the children joined me in June of 1975. We settled into a new home on Mercer Island, a predominantly white middle- and upper-income community located between Seattle and Bellevue. It was an ideal location, just across the bridge from the downtown campus overlooking Lake Washington, with a beautiful view of the snow-capped Mount Rainier. Unfortunately, the climate was very rainy, but when the sun did appear, it gave a feeling of paradise in the Puget Sound Valley.

The children enrolled in the Mercer Island Public School system. Roy Jr. was now in his junior year in high school, Kevin was a sophomore, and Crystal a freshman. Little Kelley was beginning the first grade. The children were in for a cultural awakening, being for the first time the only black kids in their classes. In Detroit, they had been accustomed to an integrated school system in a majority black school setting. Kelley often would come home complaining of her classmates making fun of her skin color and hair. The older children became concerned about Kelley being reared in an all-white school setting.

Vira enrolled as a student, pursuing a career in deaf education at the University of Washington. She was eager to finish her degree after having been interrupted by our move to Washington State. She had always been supportive of my career, having been reared in the old tradition of husband and children first.

Tensions began to accelerate at the Central Campus when I appointed two new administrators from the outside who were not members of the "old boys' network". They had worked with me within the Detroit Public Schools and Wayne County Community College system. Eugene Simms was appointed to a vacant occupational associate dean position. He was of black and Hispanic heritage. The other was a white female, Patricia Weiler, appointed to a vacant coordinator of Adult Education and ESL position.

She had worked for me as the department head for social science at Miller Junior High. She was loyal, highly capable and brought to the institution excellent credentials and experience in her area of expertise. After a short while, Weiler ran into difficulty with the old-line faculty and staff within the department. Their opposition increased with time and other emerging crises.

There was discontent among the academic middle managers prompted by an abrupt resignation of a popular Hispanic registrar. This caused a no-confidence vote in me by the managers and the unionized faculty. My newly appointed executive assistant, Carolyn Yeager, who had a close working relationship with the registrar, attempted to persuade the registrar to reconsider his resignation. Her attempt was not successful.

In the meanwhile, I met with the dissident managers to pinpoint any particular reason for their discontent. They cited unhappiness with two of my appointments and the departure of many of the old-line administrators.

After many attempts of meetings with the midline academic administrators and assuring them that I had no intent to change their roles, the group decided to take their grievances to George Corcoran, the district president. He met with the administrators without my presence and input. I advised him that he was setting a serious precedent. I perceived his behavior as a lack of respect for my position as campus president. His continuous meetings with this group caused me grave concern since I had been in the position less than a year.

The crisis resulted in an administrative mutiny, which resulted in Corcoran temporarily removing me from the campus until "a cooling off period" could determine my future at the college.

After my supervisor did not find any blazing evidence for the campus unrest, he returned me to my position. He found a great deal of fear, especially among some of the administrators who feared losing their positions at the hands of a third black campus president.

When I returned to campus, the group escalated its protest. Expanded group alliances began to form. Some members of the classified staff began to be influenced by the middle managers and faculty. To camouflage the unrest as nonracial, the group attracted some dissident blacks seeking to benefit from my demise. As a consequence, a campus-wide campaign was organized against me. I was marched around to speak to various groups to determine any inconsistencies in my remarks. When the groups couldn't find any real issues, they manufactured one: that my style of leadership was dictatorial and capricious. I remained calm and composed. I refused to give the situation power over me.

After my supervisor began to meet with members of my senior staff, my executive assistant approached me one day and said, "Roy, you have done a lot for this campus and community during your short tenure here. Why don't you seek support from those whom you have helped and befriended in the community?" I took her advice seriously since I had nothing to lose. We composed and sent letters to key community groups and business leaders on Capitol Hill in Seattle and in the central community district. The majority of the black community and black faculty stood on the sideline and observed the lynching.

The response from the Capitol Hill Chamber of Commerce, the Rev. Cecil Murray, pastor of the First AME Church and white ministers of the area provided overwhelming support. They flooded the media with letters of support and criticism of the district president's mishandling and interference with internal campus affairs. The district president had become an unpopular man with some of the Capitol Hill merchants in a stance that he had taken regarding the building of a post office in the area.

After a barrage of criticism from local business leaders, the district president announced his resignation, and all hell broke loose from the dissident factions within the campus. During the unrest, the Northwest Accreditation study team made its visit for campus re-accreditation. I met with members of the study group and assured them that job security would be provided to all of the administrators. The accreditation association re-accredited the campus, but noted in its report the level of discontent at the campus.

As soon as the accreditation team left the campus, the dissident group became even more desperate to get me removed. Corcoran continued to meet with the dissident group. He wanted me out of the campus presidency. He offered me the position of district vice president for administration. While I appreciated his gesture, I indicated that my only purpose in coming to Seattle was the presidency of the Central Campus and I would take nothing less.

I was determined to leave the position on my terms. My family and I had paid a high price: my personnel rights had been violated and derogatory comments were allowed to be aired in the media. The institution would have to pay for its mishandling of my contract.

I observed Corcoran beginning to meet privately with a black member of my senior administrative team to groom him for my removal. The senior staff member had been previously demoted from the position as dean of students by the previous president; however, upon my taking office, I befriended and elevated him to the position of dean of community affairs with responsibilities of supervising the evening school program and public relations. He was a likable and highly acceptable to the "old boys' network" of the campus by virtue of his longevity and non-threatening management behavior.

I perceived that the district president had to make the transition as nonracial as possible. This was further demonstrated as the college pitted a vocal black male faculty member against me in the news media in an article where my distracters stated, "Even the blacks on the staff are dissatisfied with his leadership." This was another bait for me to react in a negative manner.

I did not give my detractors the benefit of the "race card." I assumed the role of a true professional, remembering the advice of Big Mama "to learn from each situation that you encounter, and never allow anger or bitterness to control your behavior, but rise above the storms that will face you."

I was ready to follow the lesson learned in Management 101: "When you find that you are unable to make positive change within an institution, dust off your resume and seek other career alternatives."

I tried to shield my family from the situation, but they were exposed to all of the negative media about me in the local paper and electronic media. Vira and the children provided a level of comfort as I returned home each day. I spent many moments in meditation and quiet solitude to find peace with a God of love and forgiveness.

Leaders who head large, complex institutions are especially in need of spirituality since they face many storms, often sitting alone at the top of the organization. I had given my best to the college - it was time to show my trump card.

I hired a well-known black Seattle attorney, Philip Burton, who represented me in the negotiation of favorable terms with the district. My terms included a year's salary, professional assistance and moving expenses to seek other career options; removal of any derogatory comments from my personnel file; and a positive letter of reference to be placed in my personnel file for future references. My supervisor and board agreed to my terms.

I held a press conference in my office for the effect of high visibility to announce my resignation on my own territory. I read a brief statement of my accomplishments during my short tenure including: increased student enrollment, resolution of affirmative action issues of providing employment access and opportunity to minority subcontractors, campus re-accreditation and acquisition and implementation of half a million dollar Title III institutional development grant.

After the news conference, I walked away from the campus with two of my detractors talking to the news media, still spreading negative words about me, but I retained a positive feeling about myself and the institution, and I never looked back.

During my crises, the three older children also had learned to rise above storms in their lives. One day they came home and reported the presence of a school mascot that they perceived as a negative school image to be derogatory to people of color. The mascot was a representation of a dark-skinned Pacific Islander with a bone in his nose. It was located in a highly visible location within the hallway of the school. Kevin and his siblings wanted it removed and replaced with a better symbol to represent the spirit of the entire student body. Kevin sought our advice regarding how he could raise the level of consciousness among the students, faculty and administration to get rid of the ugly school symbol. We advised him to join the school newspaper staff as a reporter and use his pen and writing skills.

Kevin spoke out boldly with his pen, raising the level of awareness of mistreatment and unfairness to other people's cultural heritage. The stroke of his pen was sharp with scholarly criticism that resulted in the removal of the mascot. We were proud of his courage and positive leadership.

The children had been taught to respect authority, excel in scholarship, but never allow people to define them in negative terms. The incident reminded me of my early school experience when my first school principal was removed from his position by the sheriff and his deputies. I was especially reminded of the reprimand received from my father for shouting out at the sheriff as he drove by our house. It was my resolve always to stand tall for my children and to protect their human spirit under similar circumstances.

Roy Junior finished his high school education at Mercer Island High School and enrolled in the Marine Technology program at Seattle Central Campus. Since Junior High, Roy knew that he wanted to pursue a career to become a technician in air conditioning, refrigeration and heating.

The children were beginning to dislike the island as a place to live. They were instrumental in us placing our home for sale and finding a better environment for little Kelley to experience a more diversified student body. Vira and I placed the home up for sale for a considerable profit. We located a beautiful home in the Seattle Seward Park area. The home was located within walking distance of an elementary school easily accessible to Kelley. Franklin High School was located nearby for Kevin and Crystal. I had planned to stay in the Seattle area in search of other career options.

I was out of a job for the first time in my professional career. I understood the plight of black men such as my father who was constantly in search of employment to support his family. As Vira and the children were preparing to take a vacation back to Detroit, I made plans to take a quiet retreat to a small resort town along the beautiful beaches of eastern Oregon. I needed to relax, meditate and reflect upon my next career options. Upon my return, Vira and I decided to purchase a small family business with a portion of the settlement salary.

I upgraded my teaching certificate and applied for substitute teaching and began accepting daily assignments to teach science and mathematics during the interim.

My connections with the president of the black-owned Liberty Bank provided an opportunity for us to purchase a Baskin-Robbins ice cream franchise from a black owner and his wife. We made an offer and a partial payment to purchase contingent upon the acquisition of a guaranteed bank loan through the Small Business Administration.

I traveled to Salem, Oregon, established temporary residence, and was warmly welcomed by a white family to receive training as a store owner. However, within a week in training, I received an emergency call from Vira, informing me that the loan did not materialize and that I had mail from Metropolitan Technical Community College (now Metropolitan Community College) system in Omaha, Nebraska. When I returned home, I learned that I had been contacted to interview for a campus director/vice president position in Omaha. I quickly packed my bags and flew to Omaha where I was interviewed and offered the position.

My former boss, Reginald Wilson, had conducted an accreditation review of the college and its president asked him for a reference to fill a campus vacancy. My name was provided as a serious candidate, opening a new opportunity for me to return to my professional career. When I returned home and informed the family of the offer to locate to Omaha, they all said, "Omaha where?"

We placed the house on the market for sale and within a week it sold for a nice profit. We signed a six-month lease with the buyer to permit the children to finish their schooling. Kevin had finished all of his requirements and was about to graduate from high school.

I took over my new position in April 1977. I returned to Seattle in June and the family and I drove across the lofty Rockies to regroup in the rolling plains of Nebraska.

As we drove across the Western Badlands of Nebraska, the children joked that Nebraska was a place to be from and not a place to move. But within a few weeks, the family fell in love with the city and people. The state boasted its good schools, colleges and its strong emphasis on family and spiritual values.

Blacks constituted a small minority of the Greater Omaha community. Many had migrated there from the Deep South and border-states to work on the Union Pacific Railroad that had its headquarters there. Many worked at the meat packing houses and Offit Air Force Base.

The black community was concentrated on the north side with a small section on the south side near the stockyards. It was the north side of the city where Malcolm X, formerly known as Malcolm Little, was born on 24th Street. Decades later, the fires of urban rebellion would consume 24th Street during the 1960s. It also was the location of the Urban League of Greater Omaha, the Calvary Presbyterian Church, where the family later joined, and the location of the barbershop of Senator Ernie Chambers, the only black legislator in Nebraska.

I would head the Fort Omaha Campus, located a few blocks from this historic black neighborhood. The campus was a walled-in, 70-acre site, which bore an historic landmark for Chief Standing Bear of the Ponca Indians, who was confined as a prisoner in the old guardhouse building during the trial of 1879. The trial recognized for the first time that Native Americans were "human beings."

Our Native American brothers and sisters had traveled the same stormy journey as my slave ancestors in their long history in America. They had been uprooted many times to accommodate white settlers and placed on reservations, which were no more than isolated ghettos.

I felt a sense of my own history in this place. The fugitive flight of my slave ancestors had crossed with those of Native Americans. We shared the same blood and kinship. Here I was a century later as the leader of a new campus. The fort was a place where I was at peace. It provided an opportunity to regroup, re-establish my credentials and presidential image, but foremost to provide opportunities to those in need of higher education.

The college president, Marm Harris, was a southerner with a heavy drawl. I found him to be firm but fair. He developed confidence in my leadership and allowed me adequate flexibility to administer the campus. He would often tell me, "Roy, you don't allow green grass to grow under your feet." He may have had some reservations regarding my high level of community involvement, however, he never curtailed my activities in that area. I enjoyed a good working relationship with him.

I surrounded myself with an excellent team of administrators, including Robert Dunker, who helped me establish a master facilities plan for the renovation of many of the campus buildings.

Our older children were now in college and Kelley was completing elementary school. Vira had obtained employment at InterNorth (later Enron) and had many friends through her church and civic activities. Kevin had made a name for himself at the University of Nebraska at Omaha, where he had become the president of the Black Student Union. In that role, he won concessions from the college for the funding of the organization. His major in chemistry placed him in top recognition for offers from prestigious medical schools. He had maintained a 3.8 grade point average in his studies.

Roy Junior had completed his associate degree in heating, air conditioning and refrigeration.

Crystal had graduated from Omaha Central High School and had enrolled at the University of Nebraska at Omaha, pursuing a career in marketing. They were all well on their way to independent living.

During our tenure in Omaha, Vira lost her father who was 84 years old. We drove back to Muskegon Heights to join with the family to lay him to rest. Vira had lost her mother in 1964. My parents had moved to Los Angeles in their senior years.

My name had been circulated for a campus vice presidency at Miami-Dade Community College. Shortly afterward, I received a call from the district for an interview. The telephone interview resulted in a visit for further screening. I was offered the position of campus vice president of the North Campus. I accepted the position because Marm Harris had left to take the presidency of Tallahassee Community College. A new district president was appointed who did not view me as part of his new team.

The family grouped and made several decisions. Crystal had one more year to finish her undergraduate degree. She had a part-time job, so we decided to allow her to remain in Omaha. Kevin had been recruited to become a medical student by Dr. Ben Carson, the famous surgeon at Johns Hopkins University in Baltimore. We placed our home up for sale, and again Vira and three of the children remained in Omaha until the school year was over and the home was sold.

Roy Junior and I rented a truck to move part of the family's furnishings and took off in December 1980 for the long trip to Miami.

We saw a changing South as we drove through Missouri, Tennessee, Mississippi, Alabama and into Florida. We were served and accommodated by friendly white faces in motels, restaurants and gasoline stations. There were no more back doors to enter, no more white- or colored-only signs to face.

When we entered the Liberty City community in Miami, a friendly black woman named Carrie Meek, then associate dean for community education at Miami-Dade Community College, came out to greet us. Meek later became Florida's first black state representative, senator and member of the U.S. Congress since Reconstruction. Her election for these positions occurred in 1979, 1982 and 1992 respectively. She resigned from Congress in 2002.

She had arranged a rental for us next door to her home. She greeted us in a southern accent, "How y'all doing? Welcome to Miami. Come on in and rest yourselves." These comments made me feel that I had returned to my southern roots, but not quite.

The Miami-Dade Community College district enjoyed an excellent national reputation as an innovative leader in education. Its successes in bilingual and remedial education, reforms in general education, as well as its high graduation rates of its Hispanic and black students were exemplary. Still, I sensed that three issues would present a challenge to my career in Miami: urban rebellions, immigration and the condition of economic disenfranchisement of black people.

While black people in Miami had emerged from the physical shackles of legal segregation and Jim Crowism, the mental shackles still bound a large segment of the community. I perceived segments of the black community as a large elephant tied to a small stake in the ground. It would be easy for the large elephant to kick himself free, but he had been well trained to do nothing. Additionally, the white power structure at the college seemed to hitch its economic future to the goals of the emerging Hispanic-speaking immigrant population settling in Miami from Latin and Central America and the Caribbean regions.

I viewed my challenge in the following areas: getting to know the people, values and culture of the institution; assessing the needs of the campus and its service community; building a team and support system within the college and external community; establishing a collective vision and strategic direction with broad input from the campus and external community.

The college district was composed of four campuses, managed by campus vice presidents. I was appointed to head the North Campus, and a Hispanic, Eduardo Padron, headed the downtown Wolfson Campus. For the first time in Florida history, an African-American and Hispanic were heading major urban campus operations. Bill Stokes was in charge of the Kendall Campus and Elizabeth Lundgren headed the Medical Campus. Robert McCabe, the district president, was a white male who had positioned himself as a national community college leader who promoted a vision of innovation and educational excellence. His style of leadership allowed for the flexibility and risk-taking with his senior management team.

The North Campus was the oldest campus, situated in North Dade County within a predominantly black community as was the case at the Seattle Central Campus. By virtue of its location, it was perceived as the black campus even though black students were not in the majority. The college district had originated from a segregated public school system where college programs for blacks were offered in a segregated black high school, Northwestern High. A similar arrangement for white students existed in a predominantly white high school, Central High. During the early 1960s, the leadership of the college dissolved the segregated status of the college and integrated its programs in temporary facilities at the North Campus site, a former military airfield. The older, predominantly white faculty and administrative staff viewed their roles as the gatekeepers of academic excellence.

My first few months in office were devoted to getting to know the people, key players, campus and climate, programs, facilities, student body and external community. I conducted a major initial assessment of the campus to establish a vision and strategic direction.

I found four areas of concern among faculty, staff and students: a deep feeling of fear and a perceived lack of security for themselves and the facilities resulting from a recent urban disturbance in Liberty City and a number of rapes and physical assaults on campus; a declining enrollment resulting from a negative campus image; an increase in the number of under-prepared students and a need to increase academic standards to attract more eligible college students and programs; and declining physical facilities resulting from neglect and poor maintenance.

Unlike at Seattle, the more knowledgeable and experienced district president provided flexibility to build a new team of campus senior managers. This allowed me an opportunity to diversify the campus management team, including the appointment of blacks, Hispanics and women.

My team included Carrie Meek, the associate dean for community education, Dr. Daniel Derrico, dean for administration, Dr. Raymond Dunn, dean of students, and Dr. Martha Pinkston, executive assistant. The team assisted me in implementing several initiatives. Following a 1980 urban disturbance sparked by a police killing of a black insurance agent in Liberty City. We established the country's first national Community College Assessment Center for the selection, training and promotion of police officers.

Other initiatives included the construction of facilities for the training and upgrading of fire cadets and senior officers, and the construction of the Liberty City Education and Entrepreneurial Center to assist small minority businesses and Liberty City residents to take advantage of the college's broad program offerings and services. Major outreach centers were established in Hialeah and Little Haiti for the expanding Hispanic and Haitian immigrant populations.

The security climate of the campus was greatly improved through programs that trained and upgraded campus security officers. Security vehicles were equipped to provide quick response and high security visibility, and we installed security cameras and phones in strategic campus locations as well as developed security brochures for students, faculty and staff.

The image of the campus was enhanced through special events that attracted outstanding national figures to the campus, including Yolanda King, eldest daughter of the Rev. Martin Luther King Jr.; the nationally renowned photographer Gordon Parks; Earl Graves, publisher of Black Enterprise Magazine; and Steve Wozniak, one of the inventors of the Apple computer.

Outstanding baseball figures - Dusty Baker, an outfielder with the Los Angeles Dodgers, Tommy Lasorda, Los Angeles Dodgers manager, and Willie Stargill, first baseman with the Pittsburgh Pirates – were invited to campus by Physical Education Department head Demi Mainieri to play in an annual golf tournament and baseball clinic. The baseball stars also included some of our alumni – Bucky Dent, a catcher with the New York Yankees, and Mickey Rivers, an outfielder with the Yankees.

An annual memorial service honoring people who exemplified the spirit of Dr. King was launched. The program was later called the Drum Major Award for Justice.

In 1984, I was abruptly transferred to the position of district vice president for public affairs. This created concerns among some members of the faculty, staff and student body, who circulated a petition requesting that I remain in the campus leadership role. I encouraged my supporters and the community leadership to back off. I did not want to be the source of division.

I had heard rumors that I had become "too black." I later learned from a prominent black leader that my close alliance with the Cubans in Hialeah also had caused some concerns. Others reported that the president was not pleased that I had not turned around the declining enrollment of the campus.

The local black Miami Times newspaper ran a front-page article recapturing what had happened on campus, implying that the district president had wanted to appoint one of his lieutenants from the "old boys' network" to the North Campus earlier, but circumstances did not permit it. The urban disturbances had now dissipated and the time was ripe for new leadership. Two lieutenants from district management were appointed to the top two campus positions: the campus vice presidency and academic dean.

The words of Big Mama again flashed before me: "Take each hardship in your life as a challenge and rise above the storms that will face you." I moved ahead to my next assignment. I had faith that it was just a matter of time before a new opportunity would present itself.

The district president, Robert McCabe, positioned the college as the No. 1 community college in America. This designation was rendered by a study conducted by a national panel of two-year and four-year college experts who studied the college's impressive achievement record in major reforms and innovations. The college had conducted a major reform in education by raising its academic standards for graduation in its transfer program. The college led the nation in achieving the highest graduation rate of Hispanics and blacks in both two- and four-year colleges. It also provided retraining to thousands of workers who had lost their jobs in the massive downsizing and closing of the Eastern and Pan Am airlines in the South Florida area.

The new position afforded me an opportunity to initiate major initiatives including the Black Student Opportunity program, which was a partnership involving the college, Greater Miami Urban League, Mitchell Wolfson Senior Foundation, United Teachers of Dade and the Dade County Public School System. The program was a model for the improvement of high school and college completion for a selected population of black students within two inner-city public schools. The success of the program later was brought to the attention of Governor Jeb Bush, who adopted it as his Talented 20 Program for increasing minority student participation within the Florida state system of higher education at the beginning of his administration.

Other initiatives included a college enrollment management program that utilized marketing-based research strategies for student enrollment increases and retention.

The position also provided high visibility for the college to engage in community-wide programs to improve minority access to expanding business opportunities and reducing the economic disparities that existed between blacks and other groups within the county. The office initiated leadership in the creation of organizations including the Metro-Miami Action Plan and Tools for Change, both of which focused on expanding economic opportunities for blacks in metropolitan Dade County.

New challenges and opportunities began to emerge within the district. In 1984, a group of business, civic and political leaders from the city of Homestead appeared before the college Board of Trustees, requesting the establishment of a fifth college campus in that South Dade city. Acting upon their request, the Board of Trustees authorized a feasibility study to determine if the need existed. The dean of students at the Kendall Campus, Richard Schinoff, was appointed to form a team to conduct a year's study and to recommend the most appropriate action consistent with the findings of the study.

At its March 1985 board meeting, the results of the feasibility study were presented to the College Board of Trustees documenting evidence supporting the establishment of a Homestead campus. Two years later, the governor and legislature authorized the establishment of the campus and appropriated funds for planning and land acquisition.

I had been serving in my role as district vice president for public affairs for four years, and I was looking for a new challenge. One day, I summoned the college president into my office for an open discussion regarding his plans for selecting a campus vice president for the Homestead position. I asked him point blank: "Mr. President, do you have someone in mind to fill the position?" He answered in the negative. I informed him that it was my intent to place my credentials in consideration for the position. In the meantime, I also informed a number of the board members of my intentions.

A college-wide screening committee was formed, chaired by the Kendall South Campus Vice President William Stokes. I received an interview and was recommended as the No. 1 candidate for the position. The president recommended me for the appointment as the founding campus vice president of the Homestead Campus in April 1989. The board ratified the appointment.

My appointment did not come without conditions. First, McCabe indicated that I would have to relocate my residence within the Homestead community or nearby in the surrounding area. I did not understand his reasoning since he had not placed this requirement on any of my other peers who had been appointed to other campus vice presidencies. But Homestead was a small, southern town that would require a leader to be easily accepted as part of the town's "old boys' network," McCabe reasoned.

Second, I would have to accept Richard Schinoff, my competitor for the position, as executive campus dean. Schinoff, a Jewish male, was a part of the president's "old boys' network." However, I had worked with him before and did not view him as a threat to my leadership. To show his loyalty to me, McCabe told Schinoff and me together that my success was Schinoff's success.

I had been advised by some of my college friends that my superior did not expect me to succeed in the new position, especially in a town that was viewed by some as a "redneck" community with a previous history of Klan activities. Little did the president know that my roots were deep in the southern tradition, and I understood the games of both northern liberals and southern conservatives. I had learned early in my life how to get along with all people and how to handle situations of this kind.

The college received a generous donation of six acres of land from the city of Homestead and Barnett Bank to build its fifth campus.

Schinoff and I became an effective team. We spent the first year screening and hiring faculty and staff and developing the building plan with the architect. As a new leader in town, I reached out to the community to assist me. My first move was to seek the advice and wise counsel of former Mayor Irving Peskoe, a Jewish attorney with deep roots in the community. He had been a pioneer in laying the foundation for the improvement of race relations within a predominantly white traditional southern community that had a history of cross burnings and flying of the confederate flag at one of its local high schools. As a result of his leadership with others who shared his views, the community had risen to a new level of racial maturity.

My southern background had taught me that there are "good white folks" who desire to do right when the proper leadership climate is established. My mentor provided me with a list of those who would work well with me, as well as those to keep at arm's length. As a consequence, I selected a campus advisory committee from that list. This group became my sounding board for the building of a 240,000 square foot campus for the people of South Dade.

The campus groundbreaking ceremony attracted more than 300 people from the city and surrounding communities. I perceived that the district president was pleased to see the acceptance of the campus leadership in the community. My reaching out to the community placed me in a pivotal position of leadership that resulted in my election as chairman of the local chamber of commerce. This provided a platform for bringing the various racial/ethnic groups together around the issue of empowering the people to raise the level of educational standards for the attraction of new industry to the Miami-Dade South community.

McCabe organized a major tax initiative to raise $100 million through a county-wide tax referendum. But before the voters had an opportunity to cast a ballot, a major catastrophe swept through the southern end of Miami-Dade County – Hurricane Andrew. The hurricane struck during the early morning hours of Aug. 24, 1992, and destroyed everything in its path, including the temporary classroom facilities of the newly developing campus. Approximately 56 percent of the enrolled students left the area permanently.

Despite this major disaster, residents voted 2 to 1 in favor of a tax levy on their blown-away homes and businesses in support of financial assistance to Miami-Dade Community College, a great victory for the college and community.

The task of rebuilding the city, homes, businesses and the college created a new challenge for the college. A major rebuilding effort was undertaken by a coalition of residents, businesses, civic, political and religious leaders. Local, state and federal government agencies also joined. An organization called the We Will Rebuild Committee formed. The district president and I assumed a prominent leadership role in the rebuilding effort.

McCabe and the chairman of the Board of Trustees, Martin Fine met with the leadership of the South Dade community and assured them that the college would continue its efforts in building the campus in their community. The campus team and I wrote grants and assembled approximately $18 million for new facilities and programs. This was in addition to the approximately $28 million awarded the college by the state legislature. The new campus was completed, except for the new campus aviation simulation training center, by 1994. The campus became the crown jewel of the community.

The political climate of Miami-Dade Community College changed after the hurricane. The racial/ ethnic composition of the Board of Trustees changed from majority white to an ethnic minority board consisting of two black males for the first time in the college's history. Other members included three Hispanic females and two Jewish males. The board assumed a more active voice in college-related matters, especially in the area of college programs, finance and the manner in which student financial aid was administered.

Shortly thereafter, McCabe announced his retirement. Prior to his retirement, he had changed the title of campus vice president to campus president, giving the chief campus executive officer much more prestige in position.

Rumors began circulating that the Hispanic president at the downtown Wolfson Campus, Eduardo Padron, already had begun to position himself to become the next chief executive officer of the district. An article appeared in the local press that he and I most likely would become competitors for the position. I had not engaged myself with the thought of considering the opportunity to become the next president of the district, since I was nearing the age of retirement. It was my perception that the search process for the district presidency was destined to become highly political, and the potential vote of the board was not in my favor.

Despite that, I was persuaded by encouragement within the college to toss my name into the search process. I had learned that the Wolfson Campus president had obtained key commitments from major leaders within the African-American community before I had submitted my name. The local press hyped up the rhetoric by citing the number of letters of support each local candidate had received. The big media controversy came when it was reported that Florida Governor Lawton Chiles supported Padron.

My support came mainly from key business and civic leaders within the South Dade community, the black media, an Hispanic congresswoman, Ileana Ros-Lehtinen, the Hispanic mayor of Hialeah, Raul Martinez, and a prominent black state senator, Daryl Jones.

When the final vote was taken by the Board of Trustees, it was 5-2 in favor of the Wolfson Campus president. To show a united front, the two black board members voted to make the selection unanimous.

Padron was the success story of a Cuban immigrant whose family had fled Castro's communist Cuba during the 1960s. He was an alumnus of the college who had distinguished himself as a mover and shaker within the civic, education and political circles at the local, state and national levels. In fact, during the presidential search, some referred to him as an icon.

Under his leadership at the downtown Wolfson Campus, Padron had transformed a formerly low-enrollment campus into a national and international showpiece. The campus had become the home of the Miami Book Fair International, an annual literary event that attracts highly distinguished authors, playwrights, scholars and political figures from the national and international community. More than a half million people annually attend the fair.

I knew the president as a peer. I viewed him as a promoter of the college and as a shrewd power broker. He eventually surrounded himself with capable and loyal administrators to assist him in molding the institution into a new direction. He retained me as a member of his new team as campus president at Homestead.

He promoted Schinoff as interim president of the Medical Center Campus. In his place, I recommended the appointment of Dr. Alexandria Holloway, who had been the associate dean for humanities at the Kendall Campus. Holloway surrounded herself with two excellent female administrators – Stella Syracuse, facilities planner, who assisted in the completion of the construction of the campus, and Dr. Judy Lever Duffy, creator of the Virtual College.

The new district team set a new vision for the college and established a strategic direction and a new image of one college, one vision and one team with major emphasis of students first. The new direction required a series of downsizing, reforms in the general education program, a continuation of rigorous academic standards for graduation and a change in the policy of faculty governance.

The latter change produced the greatest stress within the institution. The faculty became most vocal when the College Faculty Senate was abolished and a new faculty participatory structure was put into place. The new structure provided for greater representation of the faculty from the various academic disciplines. It also provided them with greater influence on the academic programs and support services. However, it eliminated the "old boys' network" within the faculty ranks. I had attempted this change in Seattle, but the level of support above me was not in place.

However, at Miami-Dade, mutiny within the leadership of the faculty ranks resulted in the voting in of a faculty union by an overwhelming majority of the faculty. This created a strain in faculty-administrative relations to the point where faculty raises were frozen for well over a year until negotiations began. The image of the administration changed from "good guys" to "school-yard bullies." This was the Seattle experience all over again except the Board of Trustees stood firmly behind the Miami administration during the crisis period.

In March 2001, Padron reorganized the college and moved me to the district to perform as his Washington lobbyist. It was my desire to remain at the Homestead Campus to finish the construction of the aviation facility. The Homestead and Florida City councils passed resolutions to keep me there, but Padron had consolidated his power with the new Board of Trustees and saw no reason to change his direction. I announced my retirement from the college to occur on Dec. 31, 2001. I had enjoyed the challenges of leadership at four major community colleges. I was now ready to face new challenges during the senior years of my life.

I was especially grateful to the people of Homestead for accepting me as their leader and providing such an emotional sendoff. The city had risen from the devastation of Hurricane Andrew and its racial cross burnings of the past to become the true spirit of our American creed: "with liberty and justice for all."

Career in Education

Below: Seattle Central
Community College
President 1975-1976

Above: Historic Miller
Jr. High Science
Teacher 1958-1964

Principal 1969-1972

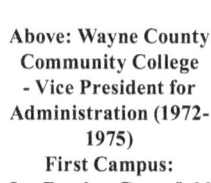

Above: Wayne County
Community College
- Vice President for
Administration (1972-
1975)
First Campus:
Joy Road at Greenfield

Metropolitan Community College Omaha,
NE - Vice President/Campus Director
1977-1980

Miami-Dade Community College
Homestead Campus Founding
Campus President 1981-2001

CHAPTER ELEVEN

The Family In Transition

Moving ahead in one's career often requires changes in geographical location. The children were uprooted several times as I had been during my childhood and adolescence. When the family left Omaha in 1981, the older children had reached young adulthood, and Kelley was about to become a teenager.

The older children had left the family nest to pursue their own careers. Kevin had entered Johns Hopkins University in Baltimore to study medicine. Roy enrolled in an apprenticeship pipe fitters' program in Miami to continue his training in air conditioning, refrigeration and heating. Crystal remained in Omaha to finish her undergraduate degree in marketing.

Kelley was the only child at home. We purchased a home in North Dade near Norland junior and senior high schools, where she easily could walk to school. Vira had taken a job as a bookkeeper with a Miami-based workshop for retarded adults.

My parents moved back to California during the 1960s. It was during this time that my father's natural father, Ellis Harris, passed away in Minneapolis. Dad's natural mother Eliza Harper/Lee had died earlier without him ever really knowing her.

Now dad was nearing retirement. He had gone back to school to obtain his master barbering license. My brother Andrew was rearing a family of his own in New Jersey and had reconciled his differences with the family.

Our family maintained a strong tradition of providing a support network for the children of relatives in difficulty. Vira received a call from her sister Vernell in Detroit informing us of problems with her oldest son. We took him under our care to assist him in the completion of his high school education. We later opened our home to two other nephews. I obtained jobs for them and assisted in enrolling them at the community college.

Miami quickly was becoming the drug capital of America with the heavy drug flow of cocaine from South America. The oldest nephew informed us that he suspected that Roy Junior was using drugs. We immediately confronted Roy about this allegation, which he denied. We talked to our nephew again, and he told us he knew for a fact that Roy was using drugs and that we should go back and confront him again. We visited again and were finally told the truth. He and his girlfriend were on drugs. We discussed the situation with them and it was decided that Roy would come home with us to see if we could assist him in kicking the habit. After a few weeks, we discovered that he was severely addicted and that our love alone was not enough to save him. He had to have professional help if he was to survive this addiction. He was still going to school and working. He had only a couple of more months before graduation from the air conditioning, heating and refrigeration program.

I located a well-respected drug rehabilitation center that would accept him for long-term care. Roy arranged with the apprenticeship director for an extended leave, but had reservations about leaving the program with such a short time before graduation. We gave him an ultimatum: either go into treatment or leave our home. The next morning he told us that he had made his decision to go into treatment.

Vira and I spent many hours with him in family counseling to help find the reason for his addiction and assure him of our love and support. Vira provided deep spiritual insight in a poem she wrote as a mother's plea for his quick recovery.

TO MY SON

"How can I tell you, how can I start
To let you know what is inside my heart?
The love, the caring, wanting desperately to help,
But knowing all along you have to do it yourself.

Was it something I did? Did I fail you somehow?
If so, I'm sorry and want to change it right now.
How can I help you save that brilliant brain
From the sure destruction of this plague called cocaine?

Try to talk it out; you know the support is here.
You have the strength, there is nothing to fear.
Talk about feelings kept deep down inside.
Bring them to the surface. Don't let them hide.

It's so hard watching your life slide away,
Trying to help you get through from day to day.
The misery, the heartache, the searing, tearing pain
Of this ever-present epidemic called cocaine.

It will consume all of you, leave you hopeless and broke.
People think it's "in", it's cool, but this is all a big joke.
Ask the users, the dealers who've landed in jail.
Ask their loved ones, their families, they'll tell the "real tale."

You can be an ordinary person or a movie star.
It doesn't give a damn who you are.
It has no regard for fortune or fame,
This mind taker, body breaker called cocaine.

Food becomes secondary. Nothing comes before

This great white "god" who always demands more.
Hold on tight, son. I know you won't fail.
One day you'll be able to tell it, "Go straight to hell!"

Hold on to your loved ones, build up the trust.
Together we can do anything, we're strong and we're tough!
So untie the ropes, break out of the chains
Of this self-destructive monster called cocaine."

After several months of intensive therapeutic counseling and family support, our son was permitted to return to his job and apprenticeship training from which he graduated with success. Roy put his life in order and moved on. He later married a young woman with deep spiritual roots. He and Deborah adopted a son, Anthony, who is now nearing his teens.

Meanwhile, our other two young adult children were experiencing out-of-the-nest pains of young adulthood. Crystal graduated from the University of Nebraska at Omaha in 1984 with a degree in marketing. She already was working at InterNorth (later Enron) part time, and was hired full time after graduation.

We were very proud of her. She was very independent and had done very well for herself after we left Omaha.

Kevin received his medical degree from Johns Hopkins in the spring of 1985. Vira, Kelley and I were joined by my brother and his younger son at Kevin's graduation ceremony. We were proud of the first medical doctor in the family.

All of the older children had been college-educated. We had sacrificed our earnings to ensure that each of them received the best education in the field that they desired. We had taught our children to take full responsibility for their own development. We always made ourselves available to help, but not to carry their load.

Kevin had announced to the family that he had a new friend whom we had expected to meet at his graduation. We were eager to meet this girlfriend whom he carefully had kept out of sight.

Shortly after returning home from his graduation, Kevin announced that he was gay. This was a great surprise. We had never noticed any gay orientation during his childhood or adolescent period. He had dated girls, but had not formed any long-lasting attachments.

Kevin's announcement was disheartening to the point of sickness: I was the father of a gay son. This had never been a known reality in the family's history. I struggled with his confession until one day Vira made me finally realize that we have no control over our children's sexual orientation. She had fully accepted it. Our children really do not belong to us; we are only caretakers. It is our responsibility as parents to accept and love them as God has placed them in our care. I acknowledged my son's gay sexual orientation by telling him that I still loved him as my son, and my devotion to him, in whatever he chose, always would be there. However, we did admonish him about the dangers of the HIV virus since it was becoming a plague in many of the large cities of America. We feared for his life.

We finally met his male friend and his mother, a very religious woman who had not come to terms with her son's lifestyle. We accepted Kevin's friend as part of our family network and loved him as one of our own. He was well educated and a good person.

Crystal had moved to Baltimore and was near Kevin as he began to experience difficulties in his medical internship at the University of Maryland. He complained of unfair treatment by a number of his supervising physicians. He cited comments made to him by one of his supervisors who said that Kevin got into medical school only through affirmative action programs that favored blacks. This allegation touched a nerve in me to the point that I boarded a plane and flew to the University of Maryland Hospital to have a conference with his advisor.

A flash from my past appeared before me aboard the plane. It was the picture of my father scolding me for shouting at the white sheriff who had arrested the principal, Jonah Parker, during my first year in school. I had made a resolve that I always would be there to defend my children in difficulty when I arrived at manhood.

After consultation with Kevin's advisor, I was assured that the program had no intent of being unfair to Kevin. The advisor informed me that Kevin was not putting forth his best effort for succeeding in the program. I provided Kevin with strong fatherly advice that the family had put too many resources into his education for him to fail or drop out of the program.

The following year, Kevin applied to do his residency at the Philadelphia College of Medicine where he completed his medical studies to become a pediatrician. He was then offered a job to practice at the Eastside Medical Clinic of Johns Hopkins University.

Meanwhile, Crystal met a young man with whom she had no common interest. She eventually married him, to the family's disappointment. The marriage lasted five years. Deciding she could take no more, Crystal left to start all over again.

The older generations were now reaching the age of transition. Mama Caroline, who had given me so much of her history, passed away on June 19, 1984, at the ripe old age of 102. She died on the same date as she had been born in 1882. I flew back to the land of my birth to reunite with the family of my ancestors.

During the spring of 1987, dad called and informed me that the doctor had found a growth on my mother's colon. I asked him to obtain a second opinion after which a second examination confirmed the small cancerous growth. If the growth was removed during the early stages, her life would be prolonged. Dad indicated that mama refused to have an operation at this stage in her life. I flew to California to be with her to celebrate her 80th birthday. When I was a child, mama always trusted me and acted upon my advice when she was ill, which was rare. I prayed and pleaded with her to have the cancerous growth removed, but she refused. She said that she did not wish to carry a bag around with her to dispose of her body waste, and if it was the Lord's will, she would continue to live. If it was not His will, her time had come.

On October 3, 1987, I received a call from dad informing me that mama had passed peacefully in her sleep. I was deeply saddened, but was relieved that she had not suffered during her illness. I gathered all of the family together to be with dad during another sad period in the family's history.

Dad had prepared for this moment. He had purchased a burial vault at the Inglewood Cemetery for both of their transitions. He also had prepared a will, outlining the manner in which his estate was to be handled. He went over all of the details with me so that there would be no questions regarding his wishes and disposition of the family estate between my brother and me.

Mama was a beautiful person who radiated love and caring for her children, relatives, friends and neighbors throughout her life. She had lived a rich and rewarding life, having been born of parents who represented the first freed people after slavery.

Dad was now alone for the second time in his life. He was nearing the age of 81. Our long African-American tradition was to take care of our parents in their old age. Although dad would be surrounded and cared for by his many relatives and friends in a neighborhood of many senior citizens, I was concerned by our long distance from him and the manner in which he would accept the loss of his mate. He kept himself occupied in his barbering career. At Christmas time, we sent for him to join in a family reunion with the family and his grandchildren.

Kelley had now come of age. She graduated from Miami-Dade Community College in 1987 with honors and decided to pursue her interest in music education at Howard University in Washington, D.C. In this way she would be on her own, but not quite, because Kevin and Crystal were close by in Baltimore. Now that Kevin had become a pediatrician, he was able to assist Kelley with some of her college expenses. In fact, we agreed that his debt to the family would be forgiven as he commenced the payment of his sister's room and board. They enjoyed a close relationship. It was ironic that they now lived in the Washington/Baltimore area, which once had been the home of their slave ancestors before they were sold into Louisiana to work the cotton and sugar cane fields. The fifth generation was now experiencing the racial maturation of America and the opportunities provided by a good education.

The Phillips

The First Family
Back row: Left to Right Kelley, Kevin, Roy Jr., Crystal
Front row: Roy Sr., Vira

The Phillips

Me and my brother Andrew

Children Seeking Mother and Father
Left to right: Tracy, Angel, Lloyd and Dexter on Angel's shoulders (1991)

CHAPTER TWELVE

The Storm Of The 1990s

After mama's transition, dad's health began to decline. He was unable to visit the family as he had in the past. He had had a heart murmur for some time. He became ill and had to be hospitalized after his 81st birthday. I received a call from his niece early one Friday morning in February 1991 informing me that dad's condition had worsened. I took an early Saturday morning flight and rushed to his bedside at the Brotman Memorial Hospital in Culver City, California. I had never seen my father in a hospital situation during all of my youth and adult years. When I entered the hospital room, he was hooked up to a heart monitoring machine. I embraced and told him that I would be there until he recovered. He was comforted in knowing that I was there with him. He wanted to talk about his plans for transitioning, but I did not want to hear about it. He insisted that I gather all of his important family documents, including his will, deed to his estate, bank accounts and burial records. I took note of his instructions.

At approximately 3 p.m. February 18, as I was about to place a call to his oldest sister in Magnolia, Arkansas, he uttered his last words: "You know what to do." His arms went up in a quick, jerky motion, and the heart monitoring machine sounded an emergency alert. The nurses rushed in and tried to revive him, but dad had made his transition.

I ran out of the room in tears, realizing that I had lost my last parent, a loving father who had cared for me since my birth. I felt lonely and sad as the nurses covered his body. I called Vira, my brother and close relatives to inform them.

I gathered the clan to join me a second time to provide a father and grandfather the last rites at the Mt. Tabor Missionary Baptist Church in Los Angeles where he had served as a founding deacon and Prince Hall Mason.

Dad was a striver, highly motivated toward self-direction and hard work to improve himself and his family. He always wanted his sons to be educated, become good men and raise their children in the knowledge of God. As a father, I tried to emulate his good spirit and be an example to my children. This was the tradition of many family-oriented black men who had their origins in the rural South.

In addition to maintaining his medical practice, Kevin had become highly involved in the Pan-African circles in his area. He attended meetings, wore African clothing, purchased a great deal of African art work and continued to exhibit his artistic talent in the study of ancient Egypt. He also traveled extensively whenever he could get away from the demands of his practice.

After the tragic death of his partner to the HIV virus, Kevin was tested by a close friend who also was a medical doctor. She informed him that he had tested positive for the virus. Although we had prepared ourselves for this possibility as best we could, it was extremely difficult to accept.

Kevin developed a deep spiritual will to rid himself of the virus through a high dependence on herbs and nontraditional medicine. His T-cell count had dropped to a dangerously low level. He confined his medical treatment to a close friend who had come into his life as an angel to look after him during that dark period.

He continued to work hard in his medical practice. To bolster his spirit, he went on a pilgrimage to view the tombs of the ancient kings of Egypt and to witness the ancient black civilizations of the Nile Valley. He came back renewed in his spirit, but realizing that his health was slowly failing him.

One Sunday in October of 1991, after returning from church, Vira called to my attention an article in The Miami Herald. She was touched by the article and accompanying photo of four black siblings - two boys and two girls. An older girl was standing between two swings with her younger brother on her shoulders and her two other siblings were sitting on swings next to her. The headline read: "Siblings in need of mother and father." There was something about the headline that moved us emotionally.

All of our children were out of the family nest, educated and well on their way into young adulthood. Vira and I were alone, standing on the shoulders of our ancestors who had struggled and sacrificed to bring us to this place.

We had purchased a home in the Goulds community near the job at the Homestead Campus. God had led us to this place to carry out a mission of lifting others as he had lifted us. Dad had left proceeds for my brother and me. My half was used to help purchase our home.

Warm memories of my father flashed before me. He had been abandoned by his natural mother, Eliza Harper/Lee, and father as an infant. He was adopted by older parents and reared to manhood. I needed to pass on the love of Big Mama and Proff Philips to another generation of neglected and abused children. We had no other choice.

The next week, we inquired about the siblings. Their records indicated that they came from an intact but highly dysfunctional family where there was evidence of abuse and child neglect. Furthermore, the records showed that the youngest girl and boy had been placed with two families who were contemplating adoption, but the adoption had been disrupted both times. They were finally reunited with their brother and sister at the Children's Home Society by the Florida State Department of Children and Families.

We started visitations to become more familiar with the children and them with us. They were happy to have all the attention focused on them. After a few weeks, we were allowed to take them out to dinner and to our home for short visits.

During the 1991 Christmas holidays, all of our own children came home as was their custom each year. The older children had a chance to meet the younger ones. We had requested and received permission to keep them most of the day. Our oldest children each purchased gifts for them and made them feel a part of their new family. We all enjoyed the holidays together.

After visiting the children for six months, we took them into our home on May 15, 1992, to await the time we could adopt them. Our four older children were matched with each of the younger children, by age and gender, to mentor and care for them in case of our passing.

At the end of May, Crystal called and informed us that Kevin had become seriously ill and would need 24-hour care. We sent for him to come home. Vira had quit her full-time job to care for the younger children. Arrangements had been made for Kevin to be seen at the University of Miami Medical AIDS Care Unit upon his arrival.

Kevin was picked up from the airport by his brother and two cousins. He was extremely frail and emaciated, bent over and moving slowly as he entered our home. We were deeply moved to see our son in this condition His energy had left his body, but not his spirit. He still felt in his heart that he could beat the virus. Once he was settled down in bed, Vira and I cried together after seeing the deterioration of our handsome son.

We became his caretakers. He was taken to the clinic each day for his treatment and finally was hospitalized. After a careful examination of his condition, it was reported that the virus had entered into his respiratory system and little else could be done to save his life. He was sent home to die. Each day I sat silently by his bedside with a nurse we hired to keep him in comfort. Vira and I witnessed the effect of the virus as it gnawed into his frail body, causing him to be unable to keep food within his system. He knew that the end was near.

On the last evening of his life, Kevin requested me to make sure an alarm system was installed in his car. He made his last request to be taken back home to be with his dog Heru. We were planning to take him home on June 20.

At approximately 8 p.m. on June 19, 1992, Kevin's condition worsened. An ambulance was called and he was returned to the hospital. When the medics arrived, he was having difficulty breathing and required oxygen. As he was being removed from the house, the children became curious and afraid. They peeked from their rooms as I climbed into the rear of the ambulance to be with Kevin. As the ambulance sped away, I sensed that this would be his last time with us.

When we arrived at the emergency entrance of Jackson Memorial Hospital, he was rushed into a treatment room. His breath of life was fast leaving him. I spoke to him that I loved him, but he could not hear. He passed slowly into the eternal darkness. Tears streamed down my cheeks in sadness, knowing that I could do nothing to bring my son back to life. I placed a call to Vira to call the family and prepare them for the sad news.

It was a strange day. It was the birthday and transition day of Mama Caroline; it also was the birthday of my brother Andrew. And it was the day of jubilee of my slave ancestors as they passed from bondage to freedom.

The family made preparation for Kevin's funeral. The immediate family gathered for a private eulogy at Woodland Memorial Park Cemetery. An African libation ceremony was conducted by the family, and Roy Junior sang "God and God Alone." A scripture was read and highlights of Kevin's life were cited. Each family member poured the water of libation into plants and cited the names of ancestors who had transitioned. This was an African tradition that Kevin had taught the family. He would have been glad to know the manner in which he was eulogized. He had truly "gone home" to join his creator and ancestors. He was only 33 years old.

We had nurtured Kevin during his early years to be a caring and loving person. He had lived a short but full life. He blossomed as a child, teenager and young adult. He was serious, studious and caring. He loved life and was an optimist, always in search of new challenges and the good life. He was multi-talented: an artist, a scientist and a humanist. He always was at the top of his class and his peers looked to him for leadership. He stood above the crowd in stature and intellectual presence but was always a part of it. He always was his own person.

His employer, Johns Hopkins Medical Services Corp., and his medical associates provided a memorial in his name in recognition of his work and his devotion to the health, education and welfare of the children of the community. The family flew to Baltimore as the clinic employees held a moving memorial and named a children's reading room in honor of our dear son.

The clouds of change began to move swiftly as other changes in the history of the family would occur. During the evening of August 23, 1992, Vira and I were holding a fundraiser at our home for the election of Florida State Senator Carrie P. Meek, who had announced her candidacy for the 17th Congressional District.

Weather bulletins flashed across the television screen announcing an approaching hurricane that was predicted to arrive the next day. I had made little preparation for the storm. Roy Junior and I made an attempt to board up windows and doors since our home had many windows and entrances. The most devastating news was announced that the storm was expected to be a Category 4 storm with winds in excess of 125 miles per hour. All families living in certain zip codes were asked to evacuate. When our zip code was called, we quickly packed essential clothing, water and food and loaded the children into the car. We headed to North Dade to Roy Junior's home because the storm was not expected to be as great a threat in that area.

Hurricane Andrew blew into the southern portion of Florida and hit land and the area of our residence around 3 a.m. August 24. The effects of the storm were milder in North Dade. The television showed scenes of the devastation in South Dade – homes, businesses, trees, telephone and electric poles destroyed beyond recognition. When we returned home the next day, our home was damaged badly. The roof was partially blown away, windows and doors smashed, the fence was blown away and debris and dead animals filled the swimming pool. The entire interior of the house was destroyed except for the kitchen, one bathroom and part of our bedroom. The home was not livable. The house was without electricity, water and air conditioning. All of the comforts that we had once enjoyed were destroyed within the span of a few hours.

The college president, Robert McCabe, and his wife Ava Park/McCabe offered us the use of their vacant home in Coral Gables until our home was fully rehabilitated. Vira and I hesitated to accept the offer. However, after considering the safety of the children, we packed our belongings and moved to the Coral Gables residence. The stay was short-lived. After a week, the president and his wife informed us that the home was being sold and offered us the use of a second residence they owned in Miami. We thanked them for their offer and decided to purchase a trailer home and live in the rear of our damaged property to properly manage the rehabilitation.

A neighborhood homeowners' association was organized to establish a night patrol to guard our homes from theft. The area had become a target for roving bands of unlicensed contractors and thieves. We also banded together to hire one major contractor to assist us in the rebuilding of our homes. We hired a black contractor who had experience in home building in an effort to support economic opportunity for small black contractors.

After approximately six months, we began to see a work stoppage. Finally, one day we confronted the contractor who admitted that he had run out of funds. Vira and I had paid two allotments, in accordance with a signed contract, totaling some $72,000. Our home was unfinished. We fired the contractor for nonperformance.

The contractor reflected the greed and unethical business practices that many homeowners suffered in the rebuilding of their homes. The two principals of the firm claimed to be a minister and a deacon, but in the final analysis, we found them to be men who were not able to honor a contract. They filed a lien against our unfinished home. After engaging a lawyer, we settled our differences and proceeded to rebuild.

The children were very unruly, having to be boxed into a three-room trailer that included two bedrooms, a kitchen and a sitting area that the girls used as their space to sleep. It was a miserable way to live.

We took the rebuilding of our home into our hands by hiring subcontractors to finish the remainder of the work. A month before moving back into our home, Vira received a call informing her that her younger sister, Delores, had passed of heart failure. Vira flew to Detroit to funeralize her sister while I attended the children.

Finally, at the end of May 1993, we moved back into our home although it was not quite finished. In any event, at least the children had enough room to run and play again. It was a relief to get back some semblance of normalcy again, but not for long. The biggest challenge lay ahead of us in rearing four children of a neglected generation, whom we officially adopted in September 1993.

CHAPTER THIRTEEN

Children Of A Neglected Generation

This chapter is devoted to the story of our oldest adopted daughter, Angel, who entered into our care at the age of nine. The other three children, Tracy, Lloyd and Dexter, were eight, seven and six respectively. Because of the sensitive nature of this chapter, the names of our adopted children are fictitious to help protect their identity. It is a most difficult story to write. It is written to share with other children and parents undergoing similar conditions. Angel died a premature death at the age of 16 after trying, but failing, to rise above the many, many storms in her short life.

Angel tells the story of what happened to her in the home of her natural parents. She wrote her story as she slowly passed away of bulimia and congestive heart failure:

"When I was a little girl, I was living in a disruptive home with so much abuse in the family. When I was a little girl my dad sexually abused me. He started to do things like at first, like to shower with me. He would rub on my private parts over and over again in the shower. Then as I grew older, he would start sticking pencils, broken broom sticks, his penis, fingers, and once the handle of a knife in my vagina. Once I was listening to music and jumping on the bed. He would call me down and stick his fingers in my private parts.

I remember a time when I missed the bus and I was home with my dad by myself. I had fell asleep and when I woke up I was tied to the bed of my parents and he put his penis in me, then when he got tired of using his penis, he stuck his fingers in me. I remember screaming.

I also remember when my parents burned my leg and when they would leave us alone at home, they would tie us up with black masking tape.

I remember when my parents was doing drugs with some friends and I begged to really go to the bathroom and I went even though my dad told me not to because of what he and my mom and friends were doing. He saw me and beat me with the buckle of a belt and left me with a scar on my right leg. I was never able to tell that these things were happening because my father kept on threatening me. He said that if I were to tell anyone that he would kill me and the family. This abuse happened from maybe age 2 to 7 three times a day everyday.

The part I don't get is when they took my younger sister and brother out of the house, why did the state leave my other brother and me in the abusive situation to suffer?"

We knew that it would take a major miracle if she were to rise above these storms. However, we were committed to giving all of them a fighting chance, a chance for change and a new life. The first item on the agenda was extensive counseling, twice weekly, for all the children. In addition, Angel also was receiving group and individual counseling at school. I reflected on her life during her seven years in our care. From the start, she was a troubled child.

Because of her severe emotional and behavioral problems, Angel was placed in a severely emotionally disturbed class. Despite her behavior, she exhibited a potential for learning, received good grades, and was especially artistic. When she entered our home, she was attending the Family and Child Development Center where she was assigned counselors and specialists to assist her in overcoming and coping with her problems. The staff was very committed and caring, which provided an excellent transition from elementary to middle school.

Angel entered her middle school years with much excitement. Her improvement in behavior and grades as she left elementary school was outstanding. The staff at the middle school was equally as committed, supportive and caring. However, as she entered the onset of puberty, a severe negative attitude began to explode within her. She developed an incorrigible attitude toward adult authority figures. This became a severe problem at home and within her school environment. Her free activities had to be restricted at home, where she frequently found herself in time-out in her room.

Within this setting, she began to seriously deface her newly purchased furniture. Holes began to appear in the walls of her room, and she set paper on fire. She was suspended for bringing a knife to school. She began to lash out at some of her teachers and counselors. Her behavior worsened. Episodes of suicide threats resulted in her placement in several hospital mental health facilities. She was not able to let go of the past and move into the future with parents who loved her. She truly was "stuck" in her old home, and all the bad memories torturing her would not allow her any peace. As a result, her behavior would not allow any peace for anyone around her. The pressure at home was mind boggling. Our household was an "Angel"-run household, consuming most of our time, thoughts and energy.

We owed it to the other children to make their environment a more peaceful one, to give more of our time and energy to them. They also had issues that were unresolved. After being taken out of their parents' home, the children were moved around a lot, and not always together. As a result, they did not seem to have a strong bond among them. They felt that Angel's behavior was a source of distraction in the family.

We finally admitted to ourselves that our love was not enough to help Angel. We made a decision to remove her, temporarily, from the home. This was a very difficult decision since one of the reasons we had taken the children was to give them a safe, secure and loving environment in which they could live together. Our heads knew that this was the right decision, but our hearts had some catching up to do. This was approximately a two-year journey, but we finally arrived at the correct decision.

We sought assistance from the After Adoption Care Unit of the state Department of Children and Families. After appealing several times before a case review panel, we were able to place her, finally, in a residential treatment setting where her educational and mental health needs could be met. It was expected that this would be temporary to allow her to return home to be with her family. During this period, the family visited with her and took part in family counseling.

Angel was nearing her 14th birthday. In her new residential setting, she was assigned to loving and caring house parents within an excellent climate for receiving schooling, social and psychological services from specialists. She had the advantage of all of the qualities of an excellent home environment.

She showed signs of improvement during our first family visit. However, as her tenure lengthened, the other side of Angel began to appear. Her counselors and teachers reported an Angel who was defiant, disobedient of the rules of the center, difficult to get along with her peers, with constant outbursts of anger. She had to be physically restrained and isolated. Her behavior required a constant transfer to different house parents.

Angel complained that she no longer wanted to be at the center. When she could no longer manipulate her therapist and others around her, she would seek a new setting where there were new faces unfamiliar with her situation. She felt the need to be a free spirit, to do whatever she wanted to do. We knew that all of this was a result of Angel not liking herself, thinking she was unlovable, that she was not worth anyone really caring about her. She felt that if she was around people who knew her, who really knew her, her cover would be blown, and they would know her for the "horrible person" she really thought she was. These feelings of inadequacy and self-loathing soon placed her on a new road.

She developed a pattern of running away from the center with other girls who had long histories of running. This was a dangerous practice of being on the streets unsupervised. During the first phase of her running, she would return before night fall.

The situation became grave when she and another girl left the premises of the center one evening and did not return. A police report was filed that she was missing. The following day, we received a call from her informing us that she and her running mate had been raped in an apartment. They were later picked up by Miami police and taken to the county hospital's rape crisis center for treatment. The police report indicated that the sexual activity was consensual since Angel's friend was closely acquainted with the boys, and they were out on a fun spree.

After her sexual encounter, Angel no longer was the innocent child that we once knew. During the next visit, we saw a different Angel. She exhibited a tough, streetwise attitude with a speech pattern filled with profanity and language unbecoming a girl of her tender age. She went downhill from that period forward, and was later diagnosed as bipolar, a severe emotional disorder causing extreme mood changes.

Through the years, we had always refused medication for Angel. We felt that drugs were being overused on too many children and did not want this to happen to our daughter. However, the situation had become so extreme in Angel's case that we gave our permission when she entered the residential center. Unfortunately, the medication made her gain weight, and this became still another problem that she had to face.

Close to a year after her placement, we noticed that she had become very lethargic and sleepy. A few days later Vira took her to Deering Hospital for a chest X-ray. Coincidentally, the technician who X-rayed her was the same one who had X-rayed her a year earlier. The results revealed an enlarged heart condition that had not been present before. This caused us great concern.

One evening in December 1997, we received a call from Angel's therapist and the nurse at the center informing us that Angel was having difficulty breathing and had been taken to Miami Children's Hospital. By the time we reached the hospital, she had been placed in intensive care under the supervision of a cardiologist. She was hooked up to a heart-monitoring machine that removed heavy dosages of lithium chloride from her body. She was diagnosed with a condition of cardiomyopathy, a severe deterioration of the heart muscles.

After being released from the hospital, Angel was returned to the residential school. Her physical and mental condition continued to deteriorate, causing her to go back and forth to the hospital. This caused her to be terminated from the program in August 1998. There were no other facilities that could handle a physically and mentally sick child.

The family was stretched out by a sick child who was unwilling or unable to cooperate in her own best interest. She was unable to attend the neighborhood school on a continuous basis because of her severe mental and physical condition. In addition to all of these problems, Angel and her younger sister Tracy began to plot to run away from home.

In January 1999, they walked away from the house without our approval and did not return until the late afternoon. The next day they each wrote a letter expressing their desire to leave home, giving no reason for doing so. On the evening of January 9, the girls climbed out of their bedroom window and did not return. We filed a missing person's report with the police department for the both of them. After they came back home that night, they started a verbal tirade against us – insults, maniacal laughter and dirty, vulgar profanity from Angel. This lasted approximately 2 ½ to 3 hours before any semblance of calm settled over the house.

The next morning, they climbed out the window again. A police report was filed again, and we sat back and waited. At around 7 p.m. a protective case worker from the Department of Children and Families came by, investigating an allegation that her "stepfather" had bruised Angel's arm. We explained the situation, answered questions, and gave him contacts from other agencies. He talked to Angel's two brothers and left. At 11 p.m. we received a call from a male caller requesting that we come and get the girls because Angel had become ill from her heart condition. I informed the person to call 911 for emergency assistance. Tracy returned home later, but only for a short while. At 3:30 a.m. the hospital called that Angel had been brought in. Vira went to the hospital and signed all the necessary papers. The attending physician was well aware of Angel's history and proceeded with the necessary paperwork to Baker Act her. She was admitted to Doral Palms Hospital later that day.

We received a call from Doral Palms asking us to meet them at Jackson Memorial Hospital Rape Center because Angel told them she had been raped. I went to the rape center at 10:30 p.m. and returned at approximately 1:15 a.m. Angel had refused to be examined after many inconsistencies were found in her story.

On January 13, we went to family counseling with Angel at Doral Palms. She refused to talk, and indicated by a "thumbs up" that she wanted to die. She was "killing" herself by refusing to take her medication and refusing food and water. She further stated that as soon as she was back at home, she was going to run away again.

On January 14, 1999, Doral Palms called and told us that Angel was going to be transferred to Deering Hospital because she was not eating, drinking or taking her medication. Vira met them at the hospital to sign her in. A few months earlier, we had learned that she was suffering from bulimia.

On Thursday, January 15, Angel came home. She walked contritely into our bedroom and apologized for her behavior. Later she ate dinner and went to bed. On Sunday, January 18, the girls ran away again, and a police report was filed again. Also on this day the protective case worker came by to talk to her again and was shocked that Angel was not at home. At the same time we were talking to the police officer who was taking the information on the girls' runaway, two other officers arrived with the girls in tow. We asked the girls to go into their bedroom for a few minutes, and when we asked them to come out, we discovered that they had climbed out the window and had run away again.

We appealed to the After Care Adoption Unit for assistance with Angel. She was returned to foster care for placement within a unit that could care for her mental and physical condition. In reality, she was a child in limbo. She would not come home without running away, and there was no suitable placement for her. She would spend time in the psychiatric ward at various hospitals. We knew this was not good for her in any way, but the other children, especially the boys, needed some relief from Angel's and Tracy's disruptions and tirades. Tracy was still running away and giving much trouble. We appealed to the Department of Children and Families to assist us with Tracy. The department eventually removed her from our home in April 1999 and placed her in Miami Bridge, a juvenile shelter, and later back into foster care. Although she never came back to our home, I visited Tracy, who was then 14, whenever I found out where she was. For a very long time, though, she did not speak to me.

Meanwhile, Angel's heart was failing rapidly. Her only hope for survival was a heart transplant, but in her mental condition (suicide threats) doctors would not recommend a heart transplant. We consented to return her home to spend the remainder of her days with the family. We placed her under hospice care with the supervision of a nurse and a home care worker.

She still ran away one final time, even in her weakened condition. She was picked up by concerned police because they said she did not look right. When Vira went to the local police station, Angel informed them that she did not want to be at home.

In reality, Angel and her sister were trying to run away from themselves. They could not tell anyone exactly where they wanted to be, but ran away from wherever they were placed. The situation was sad, grim, stressful, heartbreaking and seemingly unending.

On the morning of June 4, 1999, as I was departing for work, I entered Angel's room. She was sitting at her desk busily engaged in drawing pictures and writing stories about animals. She was in a happy mood as she turned to me and said, "Dad, see the pictures that I'm drawing?" I responded with praise: "Angel, this is good work." I placed my hand on her shoulder and said, "Good-bye. Have a good day." I departed the room and left for work, not knowing that I would not see her alive again.

At approximately 9 a.m., I received a frantic call from Angel's caretaker that the hospice nurse had arrived even though it was not her scheduled day to be with Angel. The caretaker said that Angel was having difficulty breathing.

I jumped into the car and headed home. Shortly after Vira had left home to take the boys to school, the nurse had entered Angel's room and found her resting quietly in her bed. Her eyes were open. The nurse took her pulse and found it to be very weak. She saw that Angel was slowly losing her breath.

Upon entering the house at approximately 9:30 a.m., I hurried to Angel's room and found the nurse standing by her bedside. She said in a gentle voice, "Angel just passed." My emotions swelled within me, and I burst into tears. After I composed myself, the nurse shared a letter that Angel had written to her and to the only family that had loved and cared for her through everything. The letter was entitled "My Family and Me."

Her eulogy reads:

"My family and I do lots of things together. We swim, eat at the dinner table together, eat out for meals, open our Christmas presents together, and go to the movies together if we are acting like young adults. So you can say for the most part we do things as a family. My name is Angel Phillips and I'm 16 years old. I was born in Lauderhill before three other siblings came along. So I guess that makes me the oldest out of the other three. My other siblings are Tracy Phillips who was born in Lauderhill and is 15 years old, Lloyd who is 14 years old born also in Lauderhill and Dexter who is also born in Lauderhill and is 13 years old. I also have two wonderful parents Roy Phillips who was born in Louisiana and Vira Phillips who was born in Magnolia, Arkansas. I also have four adopted brothers and sisters. They are Gene, Kevin, Crystal and Kelley. Sometimes our family is not always perfect because I'm always getting into trouble and disrupting the family most of the time. Tracy has been placed in jail for throwing a metal desk at another girl in the Miami Homestead Bridge. She also runs away from the Miami Bridge and got a pickup order on herself. Dexter has been acting up in school and is now in his room. Lloyd sometimes get his attitudes every now and then. My mother

and father can get so stressed out that they just go in
their room and think of what they can do to help us
and don't even respond to our needs at that time, but
when things get back together we seem to get along
just fine. My family is very special to me because
they have always been there for me when I'm sick,
and when I'm too weak to do anything for myself.
I mostly love my parents because they accepted
four new lives into their home with food, water, a
lot of love to give and a roof over our head. I've
always wanted to thank them for not only accepting
us into their home but for keeping us together from
splitting us all up into different homes, but I never
feel comfortable and I'm too scared too.
Mom, Dad I just want to say thank you very much
for accepting me and my sister and brothers into
your home and making us part of your life.

Written by Angel Phillips, for the family
6/1/1999

This was the spirit of God unfolding in her soul consciousness
expressing her real feelings that had been trapped in her subconscious
by the abuse imposed at an early age. Our love to her and the other
three siblings was intended to end the ugliness of child neglect and
abuse. This was our purpose in accepting them into our family.

The family prepared a family burial for Angel in the same manner
as we had done for our son Kevin. Her body was laid to rest next to
Kevin in the Woodlawn Memorial Cemetery.

The two boys found a niche to tide them through the tumultuous
middle school years and into high school. Their musical instruments
– the French horn and the tenor saxophone for Lloyd and the drums
and clarinet for Dexter - introduced to them by Vira, became that

niche. They continue to rise slowly but with difficulty above the storms of the abuse and neglect of their past. Maybe with continuous love and caring, they may reach manhood as caring adults.

Their sister Tracy, now 19, has stopped running from place to place. She resides in a foster home where her life has been changed by the birth of a daughter and a son. The Department of Children and Families has given her a last chance to continue her education and find gainful employment. We have offered to place her two children into our care until she returns to complete her education to achieve gainful employment. At this writing, she has not accepted the offer.

CHAPTER FOURTEEN

A RETURN TO
NATIVE ROOTS

During the latter decades of the twentieth century and the beginning of the twentieth-first century, some of the children of black families who had migrated out of the rural south during the post World War II era began to return to their native Southern roots. These children were now retired in the senior years of their lives. Some had gained professional status with sufficient incomes to live comfortable in areas of the south where the standard of living was lower. Many were also seeking a slower and quieter pace of life to live out the remainder of their years. Vira and I were among that group.

* * *

The old ten acres small farm site owned by Grandmother Mama Caroline and her husband, Mister James Green, had now passed on to their nine heirs.

The land was vacant and overgrown with sprouting weeds, bushes, and small sprouting trees growing beneath tall yellow pines and hardwood trees. None of the other eight heirs had expressed an interest in returning to develop their share of the land.

Vira and I visited the site during a family reunion and decided to return and build a home there. We used the sale proceeds from our

Miami real estate holdings, savings, and a portion of our retirement funds to buy out heirs interested in selling their shares. All of the heirs, except one, sold us their shares. The site was cleared by a relative who had developed a land clearance business.

We hired a local building contractor to build a 5600 square feet, four-bedroom colonial brick home with all modern conveniences. Our son, Roy Jr., came down and assisted us in our move during the fall of 2004. The adopted children decided to remain in Miami.

Vira and I became caretakers of her sister, Vernell Ingram. She had retired early from the Ford Motor Company in Detroit, due to a kidney failure. She required extensive kidney dialysis and home care. Moreover, the nearby excellent medical facilities and specialists in the Bossier/Shreveport metropolitan area provided convenience for her care.

Our return also provided Vira an opportunity to become acquainted with members of her mother's family, many of whom she had never known.

Vira's native home is located in the area referred to as the Ark-La-Tex which includes portions of Northwestern Louisiana, Southeastern Texas, and Southwestern Arkansas. She grew up approximately fifty-six miles from Minden in the small town of Magnolia, Arkansas.

Vira's visits with relatives of her mother's family uncovered information regarding her maternal ancestral roots. Information from family records revealed the history of her great maternal grandfather. He was a mulatto slave, named Alfred Boone. The family records indicate that he fled his place of birth and bondage from a plantation in Rayville, Louisiana, located in Northeastern Louisiana near the South Arkansas borders. His flight led him to Lisbon, Arkansas, a small settlement between El Dorado and Magnolia, Arkansas. He settled there and began to farm and raise a family after the period of slavery.

Like my great-great grandfather, Alfred Gooding, they shared a similar history. The two Alfreds were born around the same period between the late 1840's and early 1850's. Vira's mother, Willie Mae McGraw, originated out of the Boone-Dennis-Reynolds family line, from the marriage of Alfred Boone and Mary Reynolds.

By happen-stance, I was consulting with a lawyer, Attorney David Moore, in Shreveport. He indicated that he was a descendant of the McDade family, the slave owners of my great-great grandfather, Alfred Gooding. I asked him for additional information regarding his family. He referred me to his cousin Gretchen Benner for further information.

I visited with Mrs. Benner in her home in the Highland Community of Shreveport. She welcomed me into her home. She is a very friendly and graceful lady in her senior years.

She formerly taught at the historical Black Southern University campus branch in Shreveport. She was very eager to share information regarding the McDade family.

Her grandfather was James Germany McDade, III, born August 1, 1863 in Fannin County, Texas; and died November 29, 1940 in Caddo Parish, Louisiana. She also informed me that Buddy Roemer, III, the former governor of Louisiana, is a descendant of the McDade family through the marriage of Charles Elson Roemer II and Jolett Adeline McDade.

Mrs. Benner referred me to her cousin, Ms. Betty M. McDade of Brenham, Texas. We began to communicate by phone, e-mail, and through written correspondence. She eagerly provided a great amount of information regarding the McDade genealogical history, including sources from the McDade website: www.mcdade.bravespager.com.

The McDade European family traces it ancestry to Scotch-Irish roots in Davidson County Scotland. The group originated from the Septs, a branch of the clan Davidson, beginning somewhere in the early 14th century. The clan was apparently driven from Scotland by Oliver Cromwell (1599-1658), the Revolutionary leader of the Commonwealth (1626-1712).

The family immigrated to America, primarily to the states of Virginia, South Carolina, and Georgia. A part of the family branch eventually settled in Montgomery County, Alabama, prior to coming to East Texas and Bossier Parish, Louisiana.

Information obtained from the Bossier City, Shreve Memorial Library Historical Center reveals that the following McDade brothers settled into Bossier Parish:

James Germany McDade I (05/31/1807 – 02/28/1852)
William W. McDade (09/29/1810 – 03/11/1872)
Alexander Jackson McDade (07/28/1815 – 07/08/1880 or 1889)
Daniel Turner McDade (09/28/1821 – 01/05/1876)
Neal Franklin McDade (04/28/1829 – 08/19/1899)

Each of the five brothers was born in Montgomery County, Alabama. Their father was William McDade (04/20/1778 – 07/19/1835). William McDade I had four wives, three from which he bore sixteen children. His four wives were: Mary Germany, who bore him six children; Rebeckah Ham, who bore him one child; Rosannah Silverman, who did not birth a child; and Annabelle M. Turner, who bore him nine children.

When the five brothers and their families migrated to East Texas and Bossier Parish, they brought their slaves with them. It was a family practice to share slaves between the families. They brought their slaves into Louisiana either overland by wagon train or by boat via the Mississippi and Red Rivers.

James Germany McDade II was probable the owner of Alfred Gooding, my great-great grandfather.

Betty McDade reports that James Germany II, was born September 19, 1838 in Mount Meigs, Montgomery County, Alabama, and died September 4, 1882 in Bossier Parish, Louisiana. He fought in the Texas Confederate Army. He married Sarah "Sallie" Fort Connell, January 1, 1861 in Bossier Parish, Louisiana. She was born in Columbus, Mississippi, and died January 3, 1891 in Bossier Parish, Louisiana in the Fillmore Community, where her husband is also buried.

This information corroborates with records obtained from the history of the St. James Missionary Baptist Church. The records indicate that an Alfred K. Gooding and his wife were among the organizing families of that church that was organized in 1866 at the end of the Civil War.

The old St. James Missionary Baptist Church was located a few miles down the road, east of the Fillmore/Haughton Community near the town of Minden, Louisiana. The new church and cemetery are located in the old Concorn Settlement where many of the McDades' slaves settled at the end of the Civil War.

It is speculated that Alfred Gooding and his family remained on the McDade plantations as sharecroppers until they earned enough money to purchase an eighty acres farm from the Vicksburg/ Shreveport and Pacific Railroad company on April 7, 1887. This farm was called the "old Alfred Gooding place," located near the Goodwill Road in the Growing Valley settlement.

The McDade family is a highly influential and successful family in the Bossier Parish area. They were mainly cotton planters and members of the landed aristocracy of Northwestern Louisiana and East Texas, where many of their descendants reside today. As a result of their accumulated wealth from the planting and sale of cotton, some were able to become merchants, directors of banks, attorneys, and politicians. Many of their members are still prominent members of the Ark-La-Tex region.

Some aspects of the area have not changed. The religious life of rural Webster Parish has not changed significantly since my childhood. Services at the Growing Valley Missionary Baptist Church and other neighboring churches of the area retain the same service format. The Growing Valley Missionary Baptist church is under the leadership of a cousin, Reverend/Dr. George Rice, who has led the church into a new and much larger facility. The old Rosenwald school structure remains attached to the second church structure. The church still serves as the center of the social and religious life of the rural community.

A return to our native roots was a return to family reunion gatherings each year. Family reunions are meant to renew family kinships and recall our ancestral history and roots. It is also a time of feast and celebration for our future. While many of the families, including the Brooks, Goodings, Rices, Lees, Greens, Warrens, Hudsons, Walkers, Waltons, Smiths, Harrises, Thorntons, and Careys, scattered during the Great Migration, some of the young family members have returned to their rural family roots.

Just prior to leaving Miami, the year of 2003 ended with a sad note for me and the family. On December 26, I hurried to my brother Andrew's bedside at the Irvington General Hospital in Irvington,

New Jersey. My brother had been returned to the hospital after a long period of illness with colon cancer and complications from his diabetes. I had previously made frequent trips to be with him during this down period in his life.

Memories of our father's last hospitalization flashed before me as I entered his bedroom. He was hooked up to a respirator due to his difficulty in breathing. He was not fully conscious at the moment of my entrance; however, when I announced myself, his eyes opened in excitement. He smiled and whispered my name..."Joe". He was waiting for me to come. I wept bitterly to see him in that condition.

I spent the entire day at his bedside. He responded positively as I fed and comforted him. I prayed and meditated silently for God's presence to ease his pain and suffering. The next day, December 27, two of his boys, Andrew II and Ricky Gallman, and I bathed, shaved and placed him in a comfortable position. His condition had worsened. He refused to eat. His eyes appeared to be focused in a gaze as he fell into a deep sleep. His spirit entered into the eternal presence of God, his creator.

At 8:10 p.m., the doctor announced that he had made his transition from this earth plane. I felt alone and empty as I had during the transition of my two mothers, father, son, and daughter. I had lost my only brother and sibling. I was alone, saddened and relieved, knowing that he was out of his pain and suffering and at peace in a better state with his Maker, where we all shall transcend at the appointed time.

I remember my brother in life as a caregiver to his two families and children. He made no distinction between his four natural children and those whom he took into his care from the two marriages. He gave to his church, community, and friends from the substance of his earnings.

He loved life and had fun in it. He shared a love for learning and shared his knowledge and wisdom with others. He was a good man, once housed in a body of human frailties, some of which he had not overcome. He served his country well. After receiving an honorable discharge from the Air Force where he served in Germany and Vietnam in 1969, he was placed on disability. He took advantage of his GI Bill and returned to college. He received his Bachelor of Arts Degree in Sociology and Criminal Justice from Bloomfield College in 1981, and his Master's Degree in Sociology from Jersey City State College in 1998, both from within the state of New Jersey.

He had a special love for special education students. This led him to teach and retire as a special education teacher within the Roselle and Orange Public School systems within the state of New Jersey.

He was laid to rest with full military honors at the Fairmont Cemetery in Newark, New Jersey. He was joined by his first wife, Daisy Peterson/Phillips and their children, Ricky and Nicky Gallman, Andrew II, Jason, and Gail Caroline Phillips; and his second wife Josephine Daid Phillips and children, Deborah, Sharon, Michael and James.

Three other family members made their transition during the writing of this book. They were: Uncle S. J. Waller (1900-2004), cousin Pearlee Lee Rice Gooding (1910-2005), and cousin Hosea Gooding (1923-2003).

A return to our native roots provides a refreshing view of the natural wonders of the changing seasons. During the evening hours, Vira and I sit on the front porch in our rocking chairs and views the starry night skies. It is the same night scenery that I observed as a child on the front porch with Big Mama Lula Phillips. During the fall and winter seasons, we gaze at Hercules with its imaginary arms and legs stretching from each corner. Appearing below the night hunter, we watch the constellation of Ophiuchus – the ancient 'serpent bearer' that appears to sprawl across both the equator and the ecliptic (imaginary path of the sun) of the sky.

The quietness of the summer nights still invites the calling of night creatures from their hidden nest in the trees and underbrush. The spring of the year bring out the sweet smell of the flowers, attracting the honey bees, butterflies, and tiny humming birds. The spring showers fill the running streams and ponds that attract the tadpoles and crawfish in search of food.

The hot summer months ushers in the scorching heat of the sun rays. Missing are the long rows of cotton that were once harvested by our slave ancestors. The land is now converted into pasture land where cattle and horses wander in the green grass and sparse woodlands.

The coming of fall brings brown, red, and golden colors to the falling leaves that enriched the soil for new life to emerge the coming spring. This is the cycle of life that the creator has provided for our highest good. We have returned to the natural environment of our birth.

Vira and I have now reached the golden years of our lives. We have been united in marriage for fifty years. Our three natural children planned a golden year anniversary for us on August 5, 2007 It was a glorious and most memorable affair. Invitations were sent to many of our friends and relatives who have known us during our long marriage.

The day of the affair brought back many, many memories. I captured these memories in a tribute to her. It was entitled: "Do You Remember?" It was a recollection of how we met, raised our two families, places where our careers had taken us, and the manner in which we had spent our lives together. Our children, Roy Jr., Crystal, and Kelley, organized and produced the program. They sang beautiful songs. Our grandson, Anthony, cited the poems that he had created. He was now a tall and handsome teenager. A part of my tribute to Vira read . . .

> ". . . you continue to be that beautiful, loving and caring person, whom I met fifty years ago. You continue to be a caregiver for your sister, Vernell. But above all, you continue to put up with me . . . the same guy who fails to clean up behind himself and continues to chase after his dreams.
>
> I love you, because you are who you are. I thank God for answering my prayer: a lifelong loving soul mate; beautiful, healthy, talented children; but above all, I thank Him for you, my love and lifelong soul mate."

The year 2007 was a memorable year. It was the year I decided to run for a seat on the Webster Parish Police Jury. A police jury is similar to a county commission. It is the legislative and administrative body of a parish.

I organized a team of volunteers to support my candidacy for the police jury. The body consists of twelve representatives within the parish. I ran for district five which included the small municipalities of Dixie Inn, McIntyre, Cotton Valley, and the Growing Valley community.

My opponents were two white men from the small town of Cotton Valley. The incumbent was from an old family residing in the Cotton Valley community. The incumbent, "Cat" Cox had served in the office for many years. He had previously served as the Police Chief of the town of Cotton Valley. Like the McDades, part of his family owned large tracts of land in the Cotton Valley community.

Cotton Valley is an oil producing town. During my childhood, it enjoyed a high level of prosperity from its oil and cotton proceeds. Many of the white and black families of the town now live in poverty. The downtown community is in physical disarray. There is only one small family owned grocery store along Highway 371 leading to the towns of Cullen and Springhill.

I won the majority of the votes in the general election, but was short of a 51% majority. This forced a runoff between me and the incumbent. During the runoff election in November of 2007, I was short by five votes of winning the election.

The election provided an opportunity for meeting many of the citizens of the district. The electorate was 70% white and 30% black. I received a high level of support from white voters. I experienced a different attitude than I had encountered during my childhood. The rural South had moved to a more positive level of racial maturation, but there is still a distant to go.

The latter part of 2007 was a down period for the family. Vernell had become seriously ill, which required hospitalization at the Willis Knighton Medical Center in Shreveport. She was no longer able to care for herself. Vira and I spent many hours driving to the hospital each day to provide care and comfort.

We sent for her children and grandchildren to visit her during the long period of illness. After the visit of her children, her situation worsened. She expressed a desire to terminate any further medical treatments. She was placed in a nursing health care facility for individual care.

Similar to my brother during his long period of illness, she was no longer able to feed herself. Vira was emotionally exhausted from seeing her sister in such great pain and suffering.

On Sunday February 9, 2008, I left church and made a final visit to her bedside. I called out to her. She was in a deep sleep and did not hear my voice. On the morning of February 10, she passed quietly in her sleep.

She requested the cremation of her remains. Vira and I made previous arrangement with the Winnfield Funeral Home of Shreveport to service her remains. Vira and Vernell's children arranged for a memorial service that was held at the First Baptist Church of Southwest Detroit. Her many friends, relatives, children, and grandchildren attended, including her sons, Derrick, Craig, and Keith; her only daughter, Michelle; and her grandchildren, Witney, David, Desmond, and Cameron.

Her ashes were returned to reside in her bedroom at our home at Minden, Louisiana, where she spent her last days.

Vira and I are now alone for the first time in our marriage. The children of our first and second families are experiencing changes in their lives.

Our oldest son, Roy Jr., has turned fifty years of age. He and his wife, Deborah, and their adopted son, Anthony, still live in Miami, Florida. Anthony has grown into a fine teenager, towering over six feet. He is a junior in high school. He has become an accomplished writer of poetry and a formidable tennis player.

Deborah has earned her Bachelor's degree. She works for the Miami Police Department. Her deceased mother was a child of Bahamian decent. Deborah's grandparents immigrated to Miami from the Island of Eleuthera, which is part of the Nassau Island chain. The black Bahamian immigrants were among the first blacks to settle in Miami. In fact, because there was a shortage of white men in early Miami, black Bahamian men were the first signers of the charter to establish the City of Miami.

Roy Jr., continues to work for Miami-Dade College in his career as an air conditioning technician. He also installs and repairs air conditioning systems as an entrepreneur. His real passion is in the performing arts. He performs as an amateur actor in a small community theater and is a lead singer with a semi-professional group.

Our oldest daughter, Crystal, remains unmarried after an unsuccessful marriage. She lives and owns her own home in Bowie, Maryland, outside of the capitol city of Washington, D.C. She continues her career as a successful sales representative with the Shearing Plough Corporation. Her post-marital crisis led to a true account of how she lost nearly 160 pounds. Her weight loss led to a book: *The Me I Knew I Could Be.* Her work was highlighted in the national media: *Ebony, Essence, Fitness and Living* magazines. The *Oprah Show* and *Good Morning America* also highlighted her work.

Kelley, our youngest daughter, is now married. After receiving her Bachelor's Degree in music from Howard University in Washington, D.C., she attended the Eastman School of Music in Rochester, New York, and earned her Master's Degree in Music Education there.

She has taught music in the public schools of Miami, Florida; Rochester, New York; Silver Springs, Maryland; and Round Rock, Texas. She left her career in education and established her own vocal music business in Austin, Texas.

On November 4, 2006, Kelley and Frank Glover, Jr. of Austin, Texas, married at the Unity Church of the Hills in Austin. Frank Jr.'s family originated from Demopolis and Linden, Alabama. Frank's father, Frank Glover, Sr., served as a career military man before locating his family to Austin, Texas.

Roy Jr., Crystal, Vira, and I participated in the wedding. Kelley's best high school friends attended. Crystal served as Kelley's maid of honor. Frank Jr.'s mother, Gerlena and her daughter, Venessa, also participated in the wedding. The wedding was a high point for both families in the marriage of our two children. Frank Jr. is a fine and ambitious son-in-law. He had acquired his own home and other property holdings in the Austin community. We gave them our highest blessings for a healthy and binding relationship.

Before leaving Miami, our three adopted children were at various stages in their development. Lloyd, our oldest adopted son had graduated from high school, and achieved a $10,000 dollars music scholarship to attend Edward Waters College in Jacksonville, Florida. Dexter was entering his last year in high school. Tracey had left home earlier and failed to return due to her reluctance to live under our house rules. She had taken up residence with a young man and had borne her first child.

Vira and I sold our home in Miami and leased a house in the rural community of Homestead, Florida. We wanted to become accustomed with living in a rural environment prior to moving to rural Minden, Louisiana.

We purchased an automobile for Dexter to drive to the local high school in Homestead. One morning, he took an alternate route to school and became engaged in a fatal accident with a bicyclist. The police declared that he was at fault. The insurance company later settled the case and removed the family from further damages.

After graduating from high school in 2004, Dexter decided to enter a Job Corp training program in Kentucky. During this same period, his bother, Lloyd, dropped out of college and returned home. He had illegally obtained an automobile while at college. Shortly afterward Lloyd returned to Miami, Vira and I noticed one day that Dexter's car was missing from the yard. We approached Lloyd about the missing vehicle and he denied any knowledge of its whereabouts. We filed a police report of the missing vehicle. A few weeks later, Lloyd was arrested in the possession of the stolen vehicle. Vira and I bailed him out of jail and did not file charges against him because we did not want him to have an arrest on his record. As a result of his arrest, Lloyd lost the job that he had acquired at a local retail food chain.

After moving into our new home in rural Minden, Louisiana, Dexter did not want to relocate with us. We placed him in the care of Keith Ingram, Vernell's youngest son, and his wife at Miramar, Florida. In the meantime, Lloyd had moved in with his girlfriend and family. This was short lived. Unable to provide for her and an announced child, Lloyd took up residence with his sister, Tracy, and her new boyfriend. Unable to pay their rent, they were expelled from their apartment. Tracy was later able to seek residence in a homeless shelter.

Through the assistance of the State Department of Families and Children, Tracy was able to become gainfully employed with a large retail food chain. Her two brothers were unable to find employment. They became homeless, living on the streets of Miami. I made contact with friends and later my son, Roy Jr., to house them.

Finally, Vira and I decided to take them into our new home in Louisiana. After a few months, Lloyd became restless. One day he confronted me in an argument regarding a senseless matter involving his newly birth child in Miami. I purchased a bus ticket and sent him on his way back to Miami. Dexter obtained a part-time job in an auto supply store in Minden, but this was also short lived. He later quit his job and departed for Miami.

Dexter returned to Miami to be with one of his high school friends. He and his brother managed to obtain day labor employment, earning just enough to live in low rent housing in the South Dade area.

Lloyd took up residence with another female. We began to receive calls from the female's mother complaining of Lloyd's abusive treatment of her daughter. She indicated that he was heavy into drugs. The police were frequently summoned from his breaking and entering into their rented apartment.

In the spring of 2006, we received a call from Lloyd's female friend informing us that he had been arrested at a Homestead City shopping center for strong-arming and snatching the purse of a seventy-two year old lady. He was arrested and placed into the Dade County Detention Center to await trial for sentencing. His brother, Dexter, was now living in deplorable conditions, barely able to pay his rent. In June of 2006, I flew to Miami to teach a seminar at Nova Southeastern University. While there, I visited the three children.

I visited with Lloyd at the Metro West Detention Center. He was surprised to see me. His spirit was low. He spent his time regretting and asking for forgiveness for all of the pain that he had caused the family. He was now facing a possible ten years if convicted; however, if he took a plea, his term could possible be reduced to three to five years. I told him that we still loved him and that I would work with his attorney, Vanessa Lambert, to work on his behalf. He thanked me for my visit and assured me that every effort would be made to reform his life.

Tracy was now living in the Overtown area of Miami in a small apartment with a third child, a son. Her other two children, a female and a son, were now living with their fathers. She was still employed with the retail food chain as a stock clerk. Her apartment was empty of furnishings. She and her son were sleeping on an air mattress as a bed. It was apparent that she was not using her money wisely. After leaving her, I went to Homestead to visit with Dexter.

Dexter was living in a small room with only a mattress and an empty refrigerator near the door leading to a dark hallway. He was about to be evicted from his small apartment. Before leaving, I called the owner, whom I knew, and informed him that Dexter's rent would be paid in full within the next week. Before leaving, I made arrangement with Roy Jr. and his wife, Deborah, to allow him to live with them until better arrangements could be made. They consented.

After living with Roy Jr. for a while, Dexter expressed an interest in joining his friends at Edward Waters College in Jacksonville, Florida. The family, including his two older sisters, agreed to provide financial assistance to support his college attendance. He had a passion for drums. I arranged with the college band director at Edwards Waters to provide him with a scholarship. Vira and I signed for him to receive a financial aid loan to attend college. He enrolled at the college during the fall of 2006. Dexter and his friend visited us during the Christmas holidays. He appeared to be doing well at that time

I corresponded with Lloyd's attorney in December of 2006. We sent her Lloyd's adoption records, providing detailed information pertaining to his case history prior to his adoption into our family. I also enclosed a copy of my recently published book on the family's history, which outlines the circumstances of the children's history as part of the family. I encouraged her to utilize the information as a basis for plea bargaining to obtain a period of probation with extensive psychiatric counseling and drug rehabilitation rather than prison time. The public defense convinced the judge to provide this alternative. In 2007, Lloyd received a five-year probation and counseling to get his life together.

In March of 2007, we received a letter from Edward Waters College informing us that Dexter was no longer attending school after we had co-signed a $6,000 financial aid loan to finance his education. We later discovered that Dexter had attempted to acquire another loan through the fraudulent use of my social security number. I was forced to file a fraud alert with all of the credit bureaus.

Dexter was immediately place on notice that there would be no further financial assistance from the family. At this writing, he has dropped out of college and is currently unemployed in Jacksonville, Florida.

Our daughter Tracy now has four children. However, at this writing, three are no longer in her care. The second child has been removed and placed in the care of his grandmother by the state of Florida. Her oldest daughter has been taken by the father who resides in Jacksonville, Florida. A third child, a male, has been taken in by the father who resides in Miami. Tracy lost her job at the retail food chain where she was employed since we left Miami. Her reluctance to follow the advice of her family and others has again placed her in a very precarious predicament.

Lloyd's life has now taken a turn for the worse. He has now been sentenced to a 46 months Federal prison term for possession of a firearm.

Vira and I continue to reach out to the children, encouraging them to rise to a higher level of consciousness. The path to a better life is still opened to them as we enter a new era of change and opportunity with the election of Barack Obama, America's first African American president.

BIBLIOGRAPHY

Books

Angelou, Maya. *I Know Why the Caged Bird Sings*. New York: Bantam Books, 1970.

Douglass, Frederick and Andrews, William L. (editor). *My Bondage and My Freedom*. Urbana, IL: University of Illinois Press, 1987.

Haley, Alex. *Roots*. New York: Dell Publishing, 1977.

Songs

Boyd Jr., G.B. (secretary-treasurer). Gospel Hymns. Nashville, TN: The National Baptist Publishing Board, 1979.

Church Records

Growing Valley Missionary Baptist Church, 117th Church Anniversary, November 25, 2001; Pastor, the Rev. George Rice, Minden, LA.

St. James Missionary Baptist Church History Program, 142nd Church Program.

Wayne County Community College Facilities Master – 1978; Prepared by Howard Sims and Associates, Architects and Planners.

Court Records

Recording of the purchase of 80 acres of land April 7, 1887 by Alfred Gooden (Gooding and wife Frances Brooks/Gooding from Vicksburg/Shreveport/Pacific Railroad Co., Webster Parish Court House, Minden, LA.)

Family Obituaries

Vesta Mae Thornton at Growing Valley; Minden, LA.

McDade Family Records

Descendants of James Germany McDade, Betty McDade and Willie Griffin; McDade website: www.mcdade.braverpages.com.

Plantation Records

Bossier Parish Library Historical Center, Bossier City, LA; Shreve

Memorial Library, Shreveport, LA.

U.S. Census Records

United States Census Records of 1900 and 1910. Found at the
National Archives in Washington, D.C; Genealogical Division
of the following libraries: Shreve Memorial Library, Shreveport,
LA; Bossier Parish Library Historical Center, Bossier City, LA;
New Orleans Public Library; Miami-Dade County Library, Main
Branch, Miami.

Harris/Walker	Harris/Harper/Lee	Rice-Willis	Hamilton/Lowery	Crownover Wiley/Waller	Lowery	Phillips/Hamilton
Great-Grand-Parents	Grandparents	Great Uncle (half-brother to) George Harris	Adopted Great-Great Grandparents	Adopted Grandparents	Adopted Great-Great Grandparents	Adopted Grandparents
George (Green) Harris (1860's) and Hattie Walker (1873)	Ellis Harris (1896-1968) union to Eliza Harper/Lee	Levi Rice (1863-1941) and Annie Willis (1872-1937)	Tom Hamilton (1860) and Laura Lowery (1862)	Hardy Waller (1830) and Amanda Wiley/Crownover (1858-1941)	Robert Lowery (1840s) and Mandy (1840s) Parents of Laura Lowery/Hamilton	Proff Phillips (1863-1937) and Lula Hamilton (1877-1944)
Children	Children	Children	Children	Children		No children
Shelly (1892) William (1894) Ellis (1896-1968) Duncan (1898) Mason (1908) Susie (1904) Lena (ukn) Alice (ukn) Annie (ukn) Bessie (ukn) Luella (ukn) Maggie (ukn) Sarah (ukn)	John (1909-1991) Mary (1894) Father's half brothers And half sisters from Tom Lee And Eliza Harper/Lee Children Eugene (1891-1984) Mary (1901-1993) Rosie (1906-1994) Wesley (unknown) Tom Lee's Father And Mother were Moses Lee and Rosie Carr Sold into LA from Georgia	William (1887) Joe (1881) John (1891) Sarah (1893) Levi Jr. (1895) Annie (1899) Mattie (1899) Rosie (1905) Dellie (1906) Ellis (1904) L.D. (ukn)	Lula (1877-1944) Joe (1881) Amanda (1884) Flemie (1885) Wesley (1887) Bessie (1889) Dick (1892) Maggie (1891) Laura (1893) Ben (1895) McKinley (1898) Allie Mae (1899)	Jessie (1883) Rosie Bell (1885) Eddie (1887) Eliza (1889) Joseph (1891) Marish (1891) Andrew (1882) S.J. (1900-2004) Sidney (ukn) Pearl (1901-56) Edward (ukn) 5 others		Adopted John as only child Sam Robinson (1830) Shown in census of 1900 as possible guardian to Proff Phillips. Robinson Born in Arkansas and parents from Alabama. An uncle Joe Phillips (1847) Born in Alabama and Aunt Fannie (1852) born in LA Other children Matilda (1873) Evalina (1884) Adopted daughter Jessica (1900) Parents born in Mississippi

Brooks	Gooding/Brooks	Lee/Gooding	Lee/Thornton	Warren/Lee	Warren/Harris	Phillips/Warren
Great-Great-Great Grandparents	Great-Great Grandparents	Great-Great Grandparents	Great-Great-Grandparents	Grandparents	Great-Grandparents	Parents
Green Brooks (1827) and Lear (1835) Children Frances (1853) Benjamin (1860) Elijah (1864) Chris (1881) Melinda (1873) Bannester (1876) Maybelle (1885-1968)	Alfred Gooding (1849) and Frances Brooks (1853) Children Amanda (1867) George (1871)	Shepherd Lee (1809-1950s) and Amanda Brooks (1871) Children Caroline (1882-1984) Alfred (1898) Oscar (1893) Lear (1896) Loveina (1897) Charity (1899) Elnora (1906-1991) Emmanuel (1907-1956) Hattie (1909) Elijah (1910-2002)	Eli Lee (1850s) and Luvenia Thornton (1850's) Children Shepherd (1869) Isaiah (ukn) Anna (ukn) Caroline (ukn)	James Warren (1876) and Caroline Lee (1882-1984) Children Mary Jane (1915-1943) Mary (ukn) Dan (1913-1986) Ruthann (1915-1990) Caroline Lee and Will Green (1898-1984) Children: Lucile (1924) John (1925- A.G. (1927-2003) Thomas (1931-1993) Luther (1932- Lucy (1932- Other unions from Missouri (1917-1970's) Gladys (1923-	John Warren (1841) And Emma Harris (1858) Children James (1876) Ruthann (1888) Jessica (1892) Eliza (1904) Wesley (1896) Dan (1898) Marshal (1899) Earnest (1900's) Clem (1900) Hattie (1900's) Crissie Ann (1900's) West (1900's)	John Phillips (1909-1991) and Mary Jane Warren (1915-1943) Children Andrew (1933-2003) Roy (1934)
Great-Great Uncles and Aunts	Great Uncle					
Richard Thornton (1850's) And Sarah (1850's) Children Israel (ukn) Saformia (1882-1987) Wil (1880's) Rebecca (ukn) Effen (ukn) Tig (ukn) Charity (ukn) Mack (ukn)	George Gooding (1873) And Martha Berry (1885) Children Thomas (1894) Dell (1897) Green (1900) Honie (1902) Mattie (1909) Trudy (1909) Parilee (1910)					

574

Great- Grand- Parents	Great - Grand- mother	Grand - Parents
Joe Wilson (1840's or 50's) Jane Banks (1840's or 50's) **Children** Willie Wilson (1864) and other children Unknown	Matilda Chatman (1840's or 50's) **Children** Frankie (1870's-1950's) Sarah Chatman Cook (1863-1958) Other children Unknown	Willie Wilson (1864) and Sarah Chatman Cook (1863-1958) **Children** Hardy (1885) Wil (1888) Adine (1888-1960's) Bennett (1892) Lellie (1895) Mary (1899) Willie Mae (1907-1987)

Genealogy of Wife
Vira Phillips/Goosby
February 8th, 1938

Great Grand-Parents	Grand-Parents	Parents	Father's other Marriage	Father's other Marriage	Mother's other Marriage
Jessie Goosby (1850's or 60's) and Homan **Children** Calvin Goosby (1870's) other children unknown	Calvin Goosby (1870's or 80's) and Octavia Paschal (1880-1970's) **Children** Pierce Goosby (1895-1984) Jewel (ukn) Beamie (ukn) Odessa (ukn)	Pierce Goosby (1895-1984) Willie Mae McGraw (1905-1963) **Children and births** Vira (1938-) Pierce Jr. (1942-2006) Vernell (1944-) Deloris (1947-1993) Dorothy Faye (deceased at birth)	Pierce Goosby (1895-1984) and Homa Jacobs (born in LA) (ukn) **Children** Gena (1918-2000) Effie (1920-) Marie (ukn) Malvin (1924-) Marvin (1924 deceased) Calvin (deceased)	Pierce Goosby (1895-1984) and Lurlene Warren (ukn) **Children** Velma (deceased) Lessie (deceased) Clothiel (deceased) Male child (deceased at birth)	Murphy Paschal (deceased) and Willie Mae McGraw (1905-1963) **Children** Fannie (deceased) Augusta (1926-1999) Rebecca (1927-) Clara (1929-) Murlee (1932) Arden (1935-) Elizabeth (1936-) Jean (1937)

175

Phillips' Estate

ABOUT THE BOOK AND AUTHOR

After sixty years, Dr. Roy G. Phillips, retired founding campus president at Miami-Dade College, Homestead Campus, returned to his native home in rural Webster Parish outside of Minden, Louisiana. It took him almost forty years to fulfill a dream, a journey that began as a conversation with renowned author Alex Haley culminated with the collection of fascinating stories, and then finished in a poignant book that tells the story of his ancestors in their trajectory from Africa to America.

When he retired in December 2001, Phillips turned to writing, piercing together years' worth of research. The final product, *Exodus from the Door of No Return: Journey of an American Family* (AuthorHouse), was published in September and revised in 2008.

Phillips family saga mirrors the lives of what arguable could be the tale of most African Americans. In the book, family is the glue that binds Phillips ancestors from Slavery to Reconstruction, Jim Crow Segregation, the World Wars, the Great Migration of black families out of the South, the tumultuous civil rights period of the sixties, to the present day.

Phillips might never have started on the journey of family discovery if it had not been for a chance meeting with Haley, who had come to speak at the University of Michigan. At that time, Haley was in the midst of researching his book ***Roots***, and Phillips was completing his doctoral dissertation in urban secondary administration.

"I spent half of the night talking to him about what to do," he recalls. He said, "Go and talk to the old folks in your family. Get their stories."

Which is exactly what Phillips did. He interviewed his maternal grandmother who was then approaching her 102nd birth date. She not only recounted riveting details about her grandfather and the white family who purchased him and how he ended upon the McDade Plantation along the Red River in Bossier Parish, Louisiana.

Phillips painstaking tracked down the descendants of the plantation owners – James Germany McDade II – who owned his great grandfather and other relatives. Phillips continues to meet and correspond with the McDades in Shreveport and East Texas.

He also underwent DNA testing which helped him track both his paternal ancestry to the Mbute people in the Central African Republic and his maternal ancestry to the Mende people in Sierra Leone West Africa.

A year after retiring, Phillips was invited to Ghana, West Africa by the Honorable Christine Churcher, Minister of State for Basic Secondary and Girl Child Education, and her friend, Chief Nana Kweku Egyir Gyepi III, to assist in the development of a community college at Cape Coast Ghana, similar to the ones he had planned and managed in Detroit, Seattle, Omaha, and Miami-Dade.

While in Cape Coast Ghana, West Africa, Phillips knelt and prayed in the middle of the stone courtyard where the ancestors of many African American families exited the "door of no return" to waiting ships to be taken to the Caribbean Islands and the Americas. Prior to leaving, Phillips met with the faculty and staff at the Academy of Christ the King, a school in need of adequate facilities, educational equipment, and materials. Despite these limitations, Phillips observed a student body eager to learn. The school reminded him of the two-room segregated Rosenwald School that he first attended in rural Webster Parish during the early forties. He pledged his support to use part of the proceeds of this book to assist the children of Cape Coast Ghana in the development of its programs and facilities.

The author's impressive educational credentials include a Bachelor's Degree in Education from Eastern Michigan University at Ypsilanti; M.Ed Degree in Science Education from Wayne State University in Detroit; and a PhD in Urban Secondary Administration from the University of Michigan in Ann Arbor. He was also a National Science Fellow at Western Michigan, Cornell, Indiana, and Wayne State University.

The author has served as a secondary science teacher, an EEO Compliance Officer, and a principal within the Detroit public schools; a community college vice president and president in Detroit, Seattle, Omaha, and Miami.

Roy and his wife Vira reside at their estate in rural Webster Parish outside the City of Minden, Louisiana.

www.ingramcontent.com/pod-product-compliance
Lightning Source LLC
Chambersburg PA
CBHW021601280526
45784CB00001BA/452